Outlaw Tales of Nevada

True Stories of Nevada's Most Famous
Robbers, Rustlers, and Bandits

Charles L. Convis

TWODOT®

GUILFORD, CONNECTICUT
HELENA, MONTANA
AN IMPRINT OF THE GLOBE PEQUOT PRESS

A · T W O D O T® · B O O K

Copyright © 2006 by Morris Book Publishing, LLC

Front cover photo: "Making Their Getaway" train robbery reenactment. Denver
Public Library, Western History Collection, Z-2991. Back cover photos: Milton
Sharp, Wells Fargo Bank, N.A., and Ben Kuhl, Nevada Historical Society, Reno.
Map by Multi-Mapping Ltd. © Morris Book Publishing, LLC

Library of Congress Cataloging-in-Publication Data
Convis, Charles L., 1926-
  Outlaw tales of Nevada/Charles L. Convis.— 1st ed.
    p. cm.—(Outlaw tales series)
  Includes bibliographical references.
  ISBN-13: 978-0-7627-3983-7
  ISBN-10: 0-7627-3983-5
  1. Outlaws—Nevada—History—19th century. 2. Outlaws—Nevada—Biography.
3. Crime—Nevada—History—19th century. I. Title. II. Series.

HV6452.N3C66 2006
364.1092'2793—dc22
                                                            2006004481

Manufactured in the United States of America
First Edition/First Printing

To Mary Anne
We, too, are forty-niners. We will celebrate
our fifty-seventh anniversary this summer.

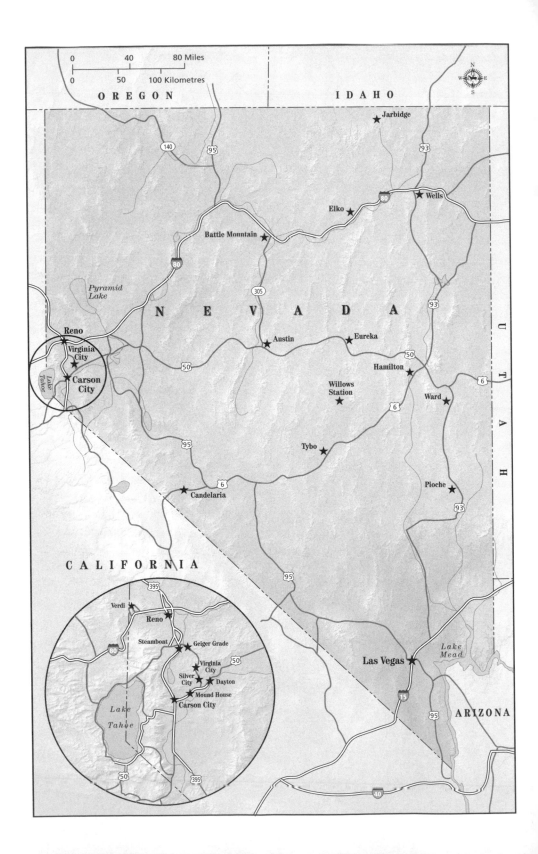

Contents

Acknowledgments

I received much assistance from the Nevada State Library and Archives in Carson City. Ann Brinkmeyer, head of technical services, and Joyce Cox, head of public services, gave me much helpful advice. Linda Poole, circulation manager, courteously and repeatedly showed me how to operate machines that weren't designed for users long on thumbs and short on dexterity. Archivists Susan Searcy and Chris Driggs cheerfully carried out many files, sometimes by the cartload, for my inspection.

Marta Gonzales-Collins, whose title is library assistant but who serves as a sort of a Jill of all trades and receptionist at the Nevada Historical Society in Reno, helped make the many hours I spent there pleasant ones. Lee Brumbaugh, curator of photographs, with his helpful hints about using a baffling array of indexes, made me glad that eight of the ten images used here came from their library.

Stephanie Hester, my editor at Globe Pequot Press, had to deal with a writer who learned WordPerfect by experience and prefers pencils to all those other mysterious electronic marvels. I thank her sincerely for her patience and gracious understanding.

——❦— Introduction —❦——

Life in the Old West was hard. Men and women had to be tough to survive. Most people brought their morality and respect for authority with them as they moved to the frontier, but some threw off much of their civilized behavior. Perhaps few in number, these misfits still leavened the mass and helped produce a lawless environment, at times approaching anarchy.

In such an environment men carried weapons for protection. Some used them too quickly; others hesitated too long. Ambiguity between right and wrong in the community sometimes showed up in an individual's own behavior. Whether one considers a person such as Wyatt Earp, Bat Masterson, Dave Mather, Jeff Milton, or Elfego Baca as lawman or outlaw depends on the incident described.

Nevada had more turmoil than most of the Old West. With a lower percentage of women and families, it lacked their ameliorative influence. But the strange circumstances surrounding the discovery of the Comstock Lode, Nevada's most defining event, would make one wonder if the Fates had cast a peculiar spell over the territory from 1857 to 1859.

Beginning with the 1849 gold rush to California, a few men saw traces of gold in streams flowing into Nevada's Carson River. Some stopped from a few days to a few years to try their luck. But they only knew about placer mining, the washing of specks of gold from sand and gravel that had to be dug out and then rocked through cradles. Running water pouring through the cradles washed out everything but the heavier gold, which could be tediously picked out. Most had no curiosity about the heavy bluish sand that clogged their cradles. They cursed and shoveled the stuff away.

Then two sons of a well-known Universalist clergyman from Reading, Pennsylvania, after poor luck prospecting in El Dorado County, California, came to Nevada to look around. Like most of the forty-niners, they were young, strong, and hard working. But they were also observant and curious, they knew a few things about chemistry and mineralogy, and they got a quiet, religious faith from their father. After a few years of saving their meager California earnings to finance their Nevada prospecting, Hosea and Allen Grosch wrote their father in 1856 that they had found a "perfect monster" of a silver vein in Gold Canyon.

In August 1857 Hosea died from gangrene after accidentally puncturing his foot with a pick. Allen considered giving up, but then he wrote his father that he would keep trying, and that his father would be entitled to Hosea's share of their discovery. On November 20, after paying off the medical and burial debts, Allen asked a Canadian friend, prospector Richard Bucke, to travel with him to California. They intended to return in the spring and develop the Grosch claims.

The winter came early and hard as it had eleven years earlier for the Donner-Reed emigrant party, just a few miles to the north. Allen and Richard had to kill their burro for food as they struggled through waist-deep snow to the summit above Squaw Valley. A second storm hit, and they could not use their homemade snowshoes in the soft snow. Six days later Bucke wanted to lie down and die, but Allen insisted on going ahead as long as they could move. The next day they took from morning until noon to crawl less than a mile. Their eyes had nearly closed from weakness when they heard a dog bark and saw smoke below them in the valley. The two men finally stumbled into Last Chance, California.

The rescue came too late. Allen died after the amputation—using a hunting knife and saw—of both legs. Bucke lost all of one foot and part of another. He returned to Canada, studied medicine in Europe, and became one of the world's leading psychiatrists.

Henry Comstock, a trapper before he became a prospector, moved into the Grosch brothers' cabin and persuaded two Indians to work the claims. Comstock was too lazy and drank too much to succeed at prospecting. But the Indians found nothing either.

Comstock, enjoying an evening ride over the hills, saw two Irishmen cleaning up their rocker. On land too barren to keep a goat alive, Comstock convinced the astonished Irishmen that he had filed a 160-acre homestead claim for a ranch, and they were trespassers.

"But I'll leave ye be if you'll cut me and my friends, Finney and Penrod, in as equal partners," announced one of the West's biggest phonies.

So Patrick McLaughlin and Peter O'Riley, to keep the peace, became partners with Comstock, James Finney, and Emanuel Penrod. The Grosch claims were thrown in with the land the Irishmen were prospecting. The town that grew out of their mining camp took its name from Finney's native state of Virginia.

O'Riley died insane. McLaughlin went to a pauper's grave. Finney, a drinker like Comstock, fell off his horse and died of a fractured skull. Penrod, who survived them all, ranched and prospected until he died. Comstock blew out his brains in a mining camp near Bozeman, Montana, and the name of the laziest, lyingest prospector in the West stuck to the richest mining lode that has ever been discovered—the Comstock Lode.

The Grosch brothers' optimism in reporting to their father about their "monster discovery" was based on at least two assays that they performed for themselves. It would be 1859 before anyone else thought of getting an assay of the blue stuff that interfered with mining gold. The California assayer thought he had made a mistake and asked for a second sample to run again. It confirmed the richness of the silver, and 1859 is the date usually given for the Comstock discovery.

After news of the discovery spread, many in North America and some in the rest of the world saw the Comstock as their wishing well. If folks could just get out there and have a little luck—or practice a little chicanery—all their wishes would come true. As the world learned that its richest mineral lode measured less than 2 miles long and only a few hundred feet wide, men and women became frantic to get their share before it was gone.

Human nature, diverse enough in quiet times, can show berserk deviations when Comstock-type events occur. Then men and women can soar to sublime heights or sink to depraved depths. On the average one Comstock miner was killed or seriously injured every day at work— work done deep in the earth, sometimes at temperatures as high as 140 degrees Fahrenheit. With that environment one should not be surprised at the violence and raw emotions that punctuated life on the Comstock.

Besides Virginia City the Comstock included such close neighbors as Gold Hill, Silver City, Carson City, the Washoe Valley towns, and Reno. This book is about outlaws in Nevada, the country's seventh largest state. But the Comstock influenced the whole state, even towns like Pioche, over 400 miles away, which had its own reputation.

My attitude toward history certainly affects my writing. But it is part of a larger attitude in a larger setting, which, in fairness, should be briefly mentioned. I think that evolutionary change in human behavior (if it occurs) would take at least a few thousand years to be noticed. So, apart from environmental influences, which we can call culture, we are no different now than the Spaniards who conquered the Incas by treachery and homicide, or the Aztecs who sacrificed their own citizens—children included—to appease their gods. I believe that Stone-Age Maoris from Australia are as intelligent as we. Some years ago, one of my sons computerized the African Games—a continental version of the International Olympics. He went on to help remote villagers around the world learn advanced computer skills, even though some of them were barely out of the Stone Age.

The first story in this book is about a bestial killer, as savage and repulsive as one could imagine. He was killed by a determined man who hunted him down and slaughtered him in cold blood. The community honored the killer's killer by making him their sheriff, I think justifiably. I have presented enough facts for you to make a judgment. You may very well disagree with Carson Valley's citizens of 150 years ago.

I have not presented both sides of an individual confrontation in the Bill Mayfield chapter. Had I done that, readers would probably be as equally divided between gambler Mayfield and Sheriff John Blackburn as the Comstock's citizens were about those two in the early Civil War when Unionist/Secessionist feelings ran high. I carried the story on through three successive and fascinating love triangles involving the killer after he escaped from custody.

Langford Peel is best known for his adventures in Montana, but the short criminal career in Nevada of this soft-voiced, steely-nerved Englishman, who had just been discharged from the United States Cavalry, justifies inclusion here. Prospectors and the men who followed them traveled often between Nevada and Montana. These territories were just four years apart in their mineral discoveries, and drifters were probably drawn to the areas because neither territory had time to develop a law-abiding society before its mineral discovery.

Sometimes one needs a sense of humor in looking at human nature in extremis. I have tried to do that with "The Perils of Rattlesnake Dick." But in spite of the light-hearted treatment in places, I am left with a strong suspicion that Rattlesnake Dick was the victim of a terrible injustice.

Many people don't know that Nevada and California were home to conflicts in the Civil War. "Bravery at Bullion Bend" shows a little-known twist in what has been called the farthest west battle of that war. Unfortunately no one has ever been able to discover the identity of the plucky girl who was a magnificent but unsung heroine in that battle.

The chapter about John Moriarty shows the explosive mix of a hot-tempered young Irishman operating in the toughest mining town in the West. After fleeing from a senseless killing in Virginia City, Moriarty changed his name and went to Pioche where he followed a strange form of outlawry—defending the owners of mining claims from other outlaws by evicting the other outlaws and then turning on their employers to drive them out, as well. After becoming a mine superintendent, himself, this outlaw faced another gunman, his rival for the affections of a prostitute. The other gunman stalked him in the streets and shot him down in cold blood.

"Train of Destiny" relates the amazing coincidence that the first two train robberies in the West happened in Nevada, *to the same train,* and *on the same day,* and there was no other connection between them.

In "Big Jack" Davis we meet an intelligent, well-educated, honest miner from California who led a Jekyll/Hyde life on the Comstock. He socialized with community stalwarts during the day and led a band of robbers with flair and flourish after dark. Like many others, he had grown tired of the hard work, exposure to danger, and privation usually needed to succeed in prospecting. Rather than return to the less exciting life he had led in the East, he turned to crime. Eventually caught, he won an early pardon by refusing to join one of the largest prison escapes in history, the subject of "Prison Riot." But he returned to crime, demonstrated his ability by inventing an unusual signaling system to know which stages to rob, and was done in by the application of a common rule of geometry.

Nicanor Rodrigues is a boy, born into the hidalgo class in Spain, who became a California outlaw at age fifteen. His daring and skill in Nevada stage robberies led to a contract in which a stage company reportedly paid him to leave them alone. However, the young hidalgo's daring and imagination were eventually exceeded by his treachery in shooting two trusted lieutenants in the back so he could escape to Mexico.

"Hunting Gold in Dazell Canyon" tells how the most professional stage robber of them all was finally captured by superb detective work. His escape from jail led to an Olympic-style journey through Nevada's harsh land, shackled and surrounded by dozens of pursuers. His later escape, after four years in prison, ended by a friend's betrayal. But investigation by the detective who had originally caught him persuaded the governor to grant a pardon.

"Prison Riot" and "A Nevada Tragedy" probably best support my ideas about human nature. In a prison break, four prison guards, two civilians, *two inmates*, and the lieutenant governor proved themselves old-fashioned heroes, but the deputy warden was a cowardly culprit.

In the last chapter, think about how changes in the times influenced what happened to the killer, to his prosecutor, and to others in the story. Also consider how good people may draw very different conclusions from the same facts, depending on positions they hold and the responsibilities attached to those positions. For example, Edward Carville served as prosecutor, as trial judge—giving advice to the governor—and as governor during this long tale of tragedy. I don't see anything in his behavior that needs apology; he prosecuted his man vigorously, he advised the governor that the man did not deserve a reduction in sentence, and then, as governor, he pardoned him. I remember what my friends from Brooklyn used to tell me in the Marines: "You pays yer money and you takes yer choice."

Sam Brown

Just Dispensation of an All-Wise Providence

About midnight on February 28, 1860, Sam Brown and Hempton Bilbo argued over a billiard game they were playing in the Gem Saloon in Carson City. Both had been drinking, and when the argument heated up, Brown challenged Bilbo to step outside and settle it. Brown wasn't known at the time on the Comstock Lode.

Bilbo, unarmed, stepped through the door first with Brown right behind. Brown whipped out his pistol and shot Bilbo in the back of his thigh. Then he disappeared, laughing as he ran away. Bilbo bled to death and Brown added another notch to a gun, well notched already in Texas and California.

Brown was nearly 6 feet tall and weighed 200 pounds. Strong and agile as a cat, he was dirty and quarrelsome, a human brute in appearance and a reptile in personality. He was slouchy, thick-witted, and slow to move until he made one of his lethal attacks. He reminded tough miners of a large lizard lying in wait for prey. He looked loathsome and repulsive; his hair was coarse, and he kept his long, red whiskers knotted under his chin. His beady eyes looked out sadistically at a hostile world.

Brown's long Spanish spurs rattled at his heels, and he carried a bowie knife and huge revolver in his belt. When people heard his booming voice, they hurried to get out of his way. Killing was to him an art form, a profession; his appetite for blood, insatiable. He intended to be the chief of all the bad men on the Comstock.

Brown had showed up in the southern Sierra mines of California in the early 1850s with a reputation of having killed several men in gun and knife fights in his native Texas. In 1853 he killed a man named Lyons in

Mariposa, California. The next year he killed three more—Chilean miners from South America—near Fiddletown, for which he served two years in San Quentin. When he was turned loose, he returned to the California goldfields, and, in late 1859, crossed the mountains to the Comstock Lode. There, Mark Twain, writing for the Virginia City *Territorial Enterprise*, said the town's first twenty-six graves contained murdered men, and Sam Brown was the worst killer of all.

Timid men ducked into stores or crossed the street when they saw the pathological killer approaching. When Brown entered a saloon, the saloon keeper dropped whatever he was doing—even if it was waiting on the richest man in camp—to see what Brown wanted. To challenge Sam Brown was to court death.

In January 1860, Sam knifed Homer Woodruff, a helpless drunk, to death in Virginia City. That May, he joined the Carson City Rangers who, with other volunteers under Major William Ormsby, rode out to punish Paiutes near Pyramid Lake for alleged depredations against whites.

The watchword and recruiting slogan of the punitive expedition was: "An Indian for breakfast and a pony to ride." Brown loved that slogan and was often heard to say, with a sneer on his lips, that he hadn't yet had his man for breakfast. Ormsby's expedition was ambushed and nearly wiped out. The major was killed, and Brown barely escaped by jumping to the back of a mule that was carrying its wounded rider away from the charging Paiutes. Brown flung the wounded man to the ground, dug his spurs into the mule, and galloped away.

In August 1860 Brown killed a man named McKenzie in a Virginia City saloon. McKenzie, a pale-faced barroom lounger, had bumped against Brown with a remark Brown thought offensive. Without a word Brown wrapped his long, gorilla-like arm around McKenzie's neck, drawing the pale face close to his own. Then, holding the man like a snake constricting a bird, he drove his bowie knife twice into McKenzie's chest, twisting it "Maltese fashion" to slice out the heart. He dropped the bleeding body to the floor, wiped his knife on his pants, laid down with a billiard-table cloth wrapped around him, and calmly sleep as the blood congealed around his victim.

Four more murders, all of misfits and castoffs, quickly and conclusively established Brown as the self-imposed chief of the Comstock's bad men. Lawlessness flourished in the mining camps, and Sam Brown reigned supreme.

Another time, Brown was working at a roadhouse when a man entered, saying he wanted something to eat. Sam pointed to a hanging chunk of bacon. "Help yourself," he grunted.

"Could I borrow your knife to cut a slice?" the man asked.

Sam pulled out his knife and then slid it back into his belt. "I've killed five men with that knife," he said, smiling strangely. "Don't know as I want to lend it out to cut hog meat."

The man left quickly and quietly. He would eat somewhere else.

Sam Brown was a bad man and, like a lot of bad men, he was also a coward. Like the lion that singles out the weakest for its kill, he selected victims where there would be no reprisals. He picked on unarmed men who had no one nearby for protection. He never attacked a man who could put up a fight. Since his victims were friendless outsiders, no vigilance committees organized to stop his slaughter of outcasts. The king of terror and mindless destruction ruled over all!

Brown confronted two determined men in his short lifetime, and they each had his number. The first was William M. Stewart, a fearless frontier lawyer who had already been California's attorney general and would later become Nevada's first United States senator. Taller than Brown and just as heavy, Stewart had left Yale to follow the 1849 gold rush to California, and he moved to the Comstock in March 1860, a few months after Brown. Stewart had piercing blue eyes and ambition to match his courage and strength. Later, he would turn down President Grant's offer of appointment to the United States Supreme Court.

On Friday, July 6, 1861, when he met Brown, Stewart was representing some mining clients before an arbitrator in the Devil's Gate Toll

House in Gold Canyon, near Virginia City. The house was divided into two rooms, a 10-foot by 14-foot bar and a 6-foot by 10-foot room behind. The hearing was being held in the small room.

Brown was in the bar when he learned about the proceedings. He decided to barge in and throw his weight around. "I'll go in there and tell 'em what's what," he announced. "Tell 'em who orter win."

Stewart knew by the voice in the bar who had demanded entrance. He wore a long overcoat with a large-bore Texas derringer in each pocket. He stepped back against the wall, pulled out the derringers, cocked them, and watched Brown stride in. At first, Brown did not notice Stewart in the small, crowded room.

"Swear me," demanded Brown.

The arbitrator looked at Stewart, who said, "Yes, please swear the witness."

Then Brown saw the two derringers pointing directly at him.

"Now what have you to say?" Stewart asked, "What do you know about the case?"

"Know about it," Brown replied. "I got me an interest in that ground."

But the intruder had little more to say with the derringers pointed at him, and his testimony soon ended.

Afterward, Brown waited in the bar for Stewart. The lawyer came out with both hands in his coat pockets, obviously still holding his derringers.

"Damn you, Stewart, I like a man like you," Brown said. "Come have a drink with me."

Stewart joined him, but kept one hand in his pocket as they drank.

"I think you and me could get justice in a mining camp," Brown said.

"You're right. We could," said the man who would later serve twenty-nine years in the United States Senate.

The next day Brown rode to Carson City to call on Stewart. He said he needed a lawyer in a suit over some rich mines he had discovered south of the Comstock at Aurora. Stewart said he needed a retainer, and

Brown said he'd be back with one in a few days. Brown rode on toward Genoa with Alexander Henderson, one of the few men willing to ride with the braggart and killer.

"Alex, today is my thirtieth birthday," Brown said, "and I believe I must have a man for supper. I've killed eleven in Nevada, and I'll make it an even dozen before sundown."

They stopped at Webster's Hotel between Carson City and Genoa, where Brown thought he'd shoot Webster. But Webster seemed ready to defend himself, so the two rode on to Genoa. There, Brown wanted to kill Robert Lockridge, but again rode on when it became clear that Lockridge would put up a fight.

Brown and his trail partner then rode on to Van Sickle's station, 3 miles south of Genoa on the emigrant road to California. Henry Van Sickle, the second man of determination Brown would meet during those two momentous days, was a German from New Jersey. He had been an Indian fighter, had been a bullwhacker in the California gold rush, and had been in the Carson Valley for nine years. By training, he was a blacksmith. He had patiently built up his station, consisting of five barns, a dance hall, a bar, several sleeping rooms, a kitchen, a dining room, and a smithy. He had mined his own rock to build the station, which was celebrated on the emigrant trail for its hospitality and for the stability and honesty of its owner. Van Sickle, a genial man and a quiet one, enjoyed the community's respect.

Brown and Henderson rode toward the dining room as the bell rang for supper. Van Sickle and M.M. Wheeler were talking on the porch as the riders drew near.

"It must be the Pony rider from Fort Churchill," Van Sickle said. "I wonders why he's so late." Among other responsibilities, Van Sickle served as local agent for the Pony Express.

"It's Sam Brown," Wheeler said, squinting his eyes. "But who's with him? I didn't know anybody'd ride with that vulture."

Brown dismounted, thinking the friendly German would not offer any resistance and would be an easy man to kill. As Brown bent to reach for his revolver, Van Sickle thought he was untying his leggings to stop for supper.

Van Sickle called out, *"Guten Abend, Herren.* You want me your horses to put up?"

"I'm not stopping with you," Brown growled. "I come to kill you, you sonofabitch. Your time is up."

Brown drew his revolver, but the surprised Van Sickle ran into the dining room before he could fire. Brown followed, but the two dozen supper guests, already seated, instinctively jumped up and milled around, thus shielding their host.

Brown shouted, "You better run you sonofabitch." Then he returned to his horse, and rode on down the emigrant road to the south.

Several guests expressed their sympathy for their host.

"I wonder why he's mad at you," one said.

"He'll be back to get you, Henry," another said. "He won't give up."

"I'm glad I'm not your insurance company."

"Get on a horse and go shoot him. There's nothing else you can do."

Others agreed that Van Sickle's life was now in mortal danger. They told him that he should arm himself and pursue Brown until he could kill him. One even offered his horse, saying he would go himself but his hand was injured and he could not shoot.

Van Sickle got his double-barreled fowling piece and decided to settle the affair at once, determined he would not live in fear of future attacks. His gun had been loaded with birdshot. Not bothering to reload the weapon in his haste, he just poured some buckshot down the barrels, and stuck two shells in his pocket. Then, he saddled and mounted a fast horse and set out in pursuit. He could hear voices of guests shouting encouragement behind him as he rode away.

Robert Fisher and a lady visiting from Placerville were riding north toward Genoa when they met Brown and Henderson about 250 yards south of Van Sickle's. Fisher heard Brown say, "I woulda killed him as quick as I would a snake if them others had stayed outa it."

After a mile of fast riding, Van Sickle had closed within range of Brown and Henderson. He shouted to Henderson to get out of the way, which Henderson did very promptly. Van Sickle jumped down, drew careful aim, and fired both barrels. He knocked Brown's hat off, although the man was not seriously wounded. Brown recovered his hat and fired two shots from his revolver as he remounted and sped away, leaving Henderson at the side of the road. Van Sickle, unhurt, jumped back on his horse, galloped after Brown, reloading his gun with the two shells he had brought with him.

Brown took refuge in the house of Bill Crosser as riders from Van Sickle's station, carrying a supply of ammunition, caught up with Van Sickle. The grim German, known for his usual cheerful manner, thanked his friends and stuffed the shells in his pocket. About this time, Henderson, riding back north, met the pursuers and said he should have shot Brown himself. "He's been raving all day about getting a man for supper on his birthday," he said.

Brown came out of Crosser's house, jumped back on his horse, and made another attempt to get away from a man who seemed determined and capable of killing him. Dusk was turning to darkness in the valley, and fear was turning to terror in Sam Brown. He rode on toward Luther Olds's station with Van Sickle still in pursuit. Van Sickle caught up with Brown at Mottsville and fired both barrels while mounted; he missed again. Brown, also mounted, returned fire three times without effect and then sped away to Israel Mott's house where he again sought refuge. By this time, the pursuit had continued for about 3 more miles and it was quite dark. Van Sickle, catching up, dismounted and watched the house. He did not want to walk toward it in the darkness.

Finally, Van Sickle asked Levi Miles, who had come out of the house, if Brown was still inside. Advised that Brown had gone out the back

Israel Mott's house in Mottsville
Nevada Historical Society, Reno

door, Van Sickle thought he might have gone on to the Olds's station. He rode there to check, but Brown wasn't there, either. While Van Sickle pondered what to do he heard spurs jingle and he recognized them as the big Spanish spurs that Brown wore. He waited in the darkness until Brown stopped his horse and dismounted.

As Brown walked toward the station, Van Sickle called out, "Sam, now I kills you."

Mortal terror seized Brown. Abject, unutterable fear sealed his lips as Van Sickle fired both barrels point blank into Brown's chest.

Then Brown yelled like an inhuman monster. His spasmodic scream of despair filled the nighttime Nevada sky, echoing back from the mountains in the west. Seven balls of buckshot were the birthday present for the most savage killer ever to terrorize the Comstock.

Other men rode up and cursed, and several of them shot into Brown's body. "Don't shoot any more," Van Sickle said. "He's dead already."

Henry Van Sickle buried Brown at his own expense. As he said later in a statement, "I saw him well buried, thus showing that which everybody knew who was in any way familiar with the circumstances. It was a necessity I would have been only glad to have avoided."

Wheeler, Fisher, Miles, and seven others testified at the coroner's inquest two days after the killing. Interestingly, Miles had witnessed Brown's trial in Mokelumne Hill, California, when he was sentenced to San Quentin for killing the Chilenos.

Miles testified that he saw Brown standing at the back door of Israel Mott's house. When the men who had been shooting at the front of the house left, Brown came out and said that Van Sickle was shooting at him and he didn't know what it was for. "He then said that another man had come up to Van Sickle's with him and asked him to go in and drink there, but he had told the man that he would not drink in any such G_d d____d man's house; also, that if Van Sickle had said anything to him he had intended to shoot him. Sometimes he would state that he did not know what Van Sickle was after him for—and then at other times he would say that Van Sickle, about a year ago, had given a man a pistol in order to shoot him."

The coroners' jury reported that Sam Brown had met his death through the just dispensation of an all-wise providence.

People came from as far away as San Francisco to thank Van Sickle for killing Brown. The community rewarded the peaceful, friendly, but determined man who had hunted down and killed his prey, and then paid for the burial. They made Van Sickle the first sheriff of Douglas County. However, in later years he often said, "No matter how justified a man may be in killing another, he never gets over it."

—————— Bill Mayfield ——————
Secessionist in Union Country

Nevada Territory divided about evenly in North–South sentiment in the Civil War. It would become the Battle Born State in 1864, and its silver wealth would help the North finance the war. But most of the working miners favored the South, while the superintendents, public officials, and business owners supported the Union. So Virginia City and the Comstock Lode, with its many miners, supported the South. Nearby Carson City, with public officials and business owners but no miners, liked the North. The division contributed to one of Nevada's most famous murders and its fascinating interstate aftermath.

Billy Mayfield, a Georgia gambler whose American ancestors came before the Revolution, hated Yankees. On August 6, 1861, he and Henry Talbot, who was usually called Cherokee Bob and was equally pro-South, got into a fight with Billy Gardner, constable at Genoa and a territorial deputy marshal. Gardner, beaten badly, survived, and Mayfield and Cherokee Bob were released on bail, pending a grand jury investigation. But the grand jury never had time to act.

The next month Cherokee Bob wounded another deputy of Marshal John L. Blackburn, a staunch Unionist, in an argument over the Gardner beating. Bailed out again, he disappeared from Nevada. We will hear from him again.

Also, before the grand jury met, Billy Mayfield had his final confrontation with Blackburn. The marshal, a tall, handsome, twenty-nine-year-old bachelor with a full beard, had been on the Comstock since the silver discovery two years before. Like most of the Comstockers, he came from California over the Sierras, the mountainous divide along

Carson Street in Carson City
Nevada Historical Society, Reno

the border. He became a United States deputy marshal, then city marshal of Carson City.

At first the dedicated Union supporter seemed quiet and peaceful in the performance of his duties. But in November 1859, he killed a man with whom he had been drinking, and the brutal circumstances led many to believe that Blackburn was the most dangerous man in the territory.

Blackburn had levied an attachment on horses belonging to George Chorpenning's Mail Service. When the marshal brought the animals back to Carson City, James Stephenson, the station keeper for Chorpenning, followed. Some said he had sworn to get the horses back or he would kill Blackburn in the attempt. But all agreed that when

Stephenson caught up with Blackburn in a Carson City saloon, the men started drinking together.

The situation that initially seemed friendly changed when Stephenson called Blackburn a son of a bitch. The marshal immediately drew his weapon and shot Stephenson over his left eye.

"I guess that will shut the son of a bitch up," Blackburn said.

Then he stepped over the dead man to set up drinks for the house and clink glasses over Stephenson's body.

Two years later, in November 1861, the Union sentiment that favored Blackburn was at least matched by the Confederate hatred for him. In that month, he came to Mayfield's home to arrest Henry Plummer, a fugitive from California.

Plummer had a checkered career in California before he became a fugitive. He also was a staunch Secessionist and close friend of Billy Mayfield. Plummer had been a marshal in Nevada County, California, before he killed the unarmed husband of a woman he was involved with. Sentenced to San Quentin for murder, he obtained his release by fraud. But two more gun battles led him to flee to Nevada where Billy Mayfield hid him in his cabin.

By the time Blackburn showed up at Mayfield's cabin with his arrest warrant, Billy had moved Plummer to the cabin of Jack Harris, another outlaw friend of his. He cut a hole in Harris's ceiling, placed a bed and food and water on the ceiling joists, lifted Plummer through the hole, and then plastered it over.

"He was here, but he left," Billy said when Blackburn showed him the warrant.

Blackburn thought that Billy was mocking him. He decided to get drunk in the St. Nicholas Saloon in Carson City. The defeat rankled him, and when he saw Billy in the saloon through his whisky-numbed haze, he accosted his adversary.

"I will arrest Plummer," Blackburn roared, "and no one can prevent it." He sneered at his antagonist and continued. "I can arrest anybody. I can even arrest you, Bill Mayfield, if I want to."

"You can arrest me if you have a warrant," Billy said, smiling softly to antagonize him. "But you can't without."

"I said I can arrest you or anyone else," the marshal snarled. "And damn you, I'll arrest you anyhow."

Blackburn made a movement as if to draw his weapon, but John Winters, a prominent citizen, and some others tried to force the marshal out of the room. Blackburn broke loose and lunged at Mayfield. Billy whipped out his bowie knife and plunged it into Blackburn's chest. Still, Blackburn moved forward. Billy grabbed the knife's handle, pulled the weapon out, and stabbed his drunken opponent again and again. After a half dozen stabs, the marshal slumped to the floor and bled to death within ten minutes.

In the excitement Mayfield escaped from the room. He lay hidden all night in a hog pen. Friends found him and hid him in more fragrant quarters. But a $4,000 reward convinced someone to turn him in, and he was taken into custody.

Billy Mayfield, aware that he would be tried as much for being a Secessionist in a union county as for killing the marshal, knew he had to escape. When a female friend visited, she brought a small saw in her stocking. Billy had sawed through the rivets of his leg irons and was removing them when a guard, looking through the "Judas hole" discovered what had happened. The jailer kept quiet and allowed the friend another visit. This time a body search revealed two small files concealed in her stocking. They arrested the woman and increased security by putting Billy under a heavy guard.

Feelings in the community ran high with the ardent Secessionist killing the loyal Unionist. Governor Nye requested federal help, and the commandant at nearby Fort Churchill sent fifty soldiers to guard the prisoner. John O'Connell, a distinguished Secessionist who had just been defeated for governor of California, and Jonas Seely, an equally pronounced Unionist, served as counsel for Mayfield. After a trial that took most of January, the jury returned a guilty verdict, and Mayfield was sentenced to hang on February 28, 1862. Billy claimed that he had been denied a fair trial because there was not a single Democrat on the jury.

There were men of both political parties who had no interest in the case other than relief that Blackburn was dead, and they felt gratitude toward his slayer. Through their efforts, two of the judges of the Territorial Supreme Court ordered a stay of proceedings until the case could be brought before the whole court. This rendered the time of execution uncertain, and the authorities decided to dispense with the military guard and transfer Mayfield to the territorial prison, which shared the same building as the Warm Springs Hotel in Carson City.

Abe Curry, the prison warden, was a good man, kind-hearted and public spirited. He also liked to play poker. Mayfield's female friend smuggled in the necessary tools, and Billy sawed through the rivets of his legirons. Other friends waited outside on the night of March 15, 1862, with $1,000 and a fast horse.

Mayfield later recalled his escape: "The guard was walking back and forth in the wardroom, while old man Curry was sitting playing poker with some of his work hands about ten feet from my cell. I got down on my knees, and, watching the old man's eyes, started for the door. As I got to it I saw the old man raising the hand that had just been dealt to him, and, as his eyes were directed toward me, I thought I would wait until he got a big hand, for, being an old gambler myself, I knew it would always excite an unsophisticated gambler to have a big hand dealt to him. A few minutes afterward a big Irishman who was playing in the game got a big hand —queens and sevens before the draw. He bet twenty beans; the old man saw it, and they took one card each. The old man drew a king, making him a king full; the Irishman drew a queen, making him a queen full. They bet and bet until they had about 200 beans in the pot. All this time I was fixing to go, and I came to the conclusion that if I could not go out on that hand I never could, and so I went."

Mayfield rode north, crossed the Truckee River, and was well up the Peavine Valley into California before he finally stopped. Every mile was separating him from the Carson City girl with whom he was in love. The terrible conflict raged for a time and then the love of a woman outweighed the love of freedom. He turned back to the house of friends, the Huffakers in the Washoe Valley, about 20 miles from Carson City.

He remained there about two weeks, regularly communicating with his sweetheart, as more and more people seemed to learn of his whereabouts. Friends urged him to move on. The new marshal even came once. Not wishing to show ingratitude to the man who created the vacancy that he had filled, Marshal D. J. Gasherie informed Billy's friends of the time he planned to visit. Billy paid no attention to the warnings of his friends, so he was there when Gasherie arrived.

Mrs. Huffaker quickly concealed Billy behind some dresses hanging along a wall. Gasherie searched the house from cellar to loft without success. Apparently, he did see a pair of boots protruding from under a jewel-spangled dress in the closet. Later, Gasherie said, "I couldn't find him, but it seemed like I could see him all over."

Finally, Billy's friends convinced him to leave, and he rode to present-day Idaho, where he joined friends Henry Plummer and Cherokee Bob Talbot. He teamed up with Cherokee Bob in Lewiston and resumed gambling. Bob was in love with Cynthia, a charming redheaded divorcee who worked as a hostess in the Luna House Hotel. When Billy saw Cynthia, he forgot all about the Carson City sweetheart.

At first Billy and Bob ignored the love triangle, hoping it would resolve itself. Then, the discovery of gold on the Salmon River in June 1862 provided a distraction. They moved 100 miles to the new mining camp at Florence, set up their gambling establishment in a log cabin at the end of the main street, and got a smaller cabin for the private residence of their mutual love.

The gambling saloon flourished, but the love situation grew more intense. By fall it was intolerable. Both men were friends and wanted to avoid gunplay, so they agreed to let Cynthia choose. To the surprise of both men, she chose Cherokee Bob. Bob had recently acquired a second saloon at the Oro Fino camp, and some cynics thought his financial prospects influenced the lady's decision, particularly since she cried hard at leaving Billy.

Like a good gambler, Billy concealed his disappointment and offered his share of the business to the lovers. Bob, as elated as he was surprised, insisted on paying in full for Billy's half of the saloon. They parted as friends. Billy's parting from Florence was another matter.

Miners were already leaving Florence, either to go home or to try another gold camp. Billy, annoyed with the Union sentiment in Idaho, decided to make his an auspicious departure. He invited every rebel sympathizer who could borrow or steal a horse to come and join the farewell party.

On October 6, 1862, exactly at 9:00 P.M., Colonel Mayfield and his motley cavalry swept into Florence with raucous cheers for Jeff Davis and the Confederacy. They dismounted long enough to plunder the enemy saloons, restaurants, stores, and hotels, and then they galloped off into the night. Mayfield settled at Placerville on Grimes Creek, north of present-day Boise.

Cherokee Bob's romantic troubles were not resolved by Billy's departure to the Boise area. Jakey Williams, Cynthia's previous husband whom she had divorced, also ran a saloon in Florence. With Billy out of the picture, Jakey felt freer to denounce his former wife's present lover as a rebel bastard. He also sneered that Bob was a half-breed, since Bob's mother, whom he worshiped, was a full-blooded Cherokee. The conflict intensified and came to a head on the last day of 1862.

Jakey helped plan the New Year's Eve ball, which Cynthia wanted to attend. Expecting heavy betting, Bob did not want to take the evening off. He got his fellow Georgian, Red Face Bill, to escort Cynthia to the dance. He impressed on Cynthia's partner for the evening that she was to be treated decently. "If things don't go right," Bob said, "just report to me."

Cynthia, dressed for mining camp balls and glittering with jewelry, arrived fashionably late with Red Face Bill. Jakey, on the watch, intercepted them as soon as they arrived. "You'll have to take her home," he said.

Red Face Bill, outnumbered by the largely Unionist party, quietly complied. Cynthia cried. She not only missed the party but felt that she had been singled out as a social outcast. An outraged Cherokee Bob swore revenge.

Jakey avoided Bob for one day, but on January 2, 1863, Bob issued a direct challenge. Jakey grabbed his shotgun and marched through the snow to Bob's saloon. Friends joined behind him until he led a small posse. The shootout lasted only a few minutes. When it ended, Red Face Bill lay dead with blood pouring out into the snow from fourteen wounds. Cherokee Bob, with five wounds, was still alive.

Bob clung to life for three days, pleading with Cynthia to follow Mayfield to the Boise area and reunite with him. Bob mistakenly believed that he had killed Jakey, and Cynthia did not wound his pride by telling otherwise. Cherokee Bob's last words show the pride in what he thought was his newly arrived status and also that he was thinking of his Indian heritage. He said to Cynthia, "Tell my brother that I have killed my man, and gone on a long hunt."

After the coroner's inquest, the justice of the peace held that Jakey and the other man who fired the fatal shots were both acting in self-defense. He said the men who died with nineteen bullet wounds between them had attacked the leaders of the posse with intent to kill.

With Cherokee Bob's death, the third love triangle fell into place. Cynthia kept her vow to Bob and found Mayfield at Placerville, on Grimes Creek, near present Boise. Jakey followed, but Mayfield, enjoying a great run of luck, was now worth about $50,000. Jakey, unable to compete with those figures, found himself another wife.

In spring of 1863, Mayfield was dealing cards when one of the players, a man named Evans, complained. They argued a while and Mayfield drew his revolver.

"I'm not heeled," Evans said.

"Then go heel yourself," Mayfield replied. "Be ready next time we meet. One of us must die."

The next day Mayfield and two friends walked along a muddy street and came to a place where they had to cross in single file on a plank. Evans, armed with a double-barreled shotgun, lay in ambush. When Mayfield was alone in the center of the plank, Evans fired both barrels of buckshot into his body. Mayfield grabbed for his revolver, but fell into the mud before he could draw it. Within a few minutes, the man who came near to involving Nevada Territory in civil warfare, lay dead in the street.

Cynthia mourned her lover for a time and then became a prostitute. The charms that attracted Billy Mayfield, Cherokee Bob, and Jakey Williams to her continued to win admirers. Some say she caused more separations, quarrels, and deaths than any other woman in the Rocky Mountains.

Langford Farner Peel
His "Redeemer" Never Came

When Sam Brown departed this world with a double load of buckshot in his chest, other gunmen sought recognition as chief of the Comstock. After several months passed without resolution of the matter, Johnny Dennis, usually called El Dorado Johnny, decided to make his move. He knew that Langford Farner Peel had recently arrived from Salt Lake City with a record of five killings in that City of the Saints.

Peel, a tall, slender, handsome man with a soft voice, had been raised in England. He had served two enlistments in the United States Cavalry, the second one bringing him to Salt Lake City, where he was discharged after a vicious fight with another soldier. He was a golden man with golden hair, a golden beard, and wide blue eyes that suggested gentleness. But he was gentle only when sober. In his cups, he could be a hound from hell.

A few months before El Dorado Johnny got his idea, Dick Paddock had a "discussion" with Peel in Robinson and Gentry's saloon in Virginia City. After a few harsh words passed, Paddock asked, "Do you want to take that up?"

"I haven't any objection," Peel replied in his quiet way.

"Very well, what's your game?" Paddock asked.

"Your game is mine. You choose."

They walked outside, took up positions, and opened fire. Paddock shot first. His shot missed, and Peel took careful aim, hitting Paddock's gun hand. Then he shot Paddock in the chest, a wound from which he recovered. Paddock's second and third shots were even wilder than the first, and Peel suffered no injury.

Peel's coolness under fire was the talk of Virginia City, and El Dorado Johnny knew where to start his campaign for chief of the Comstock. On October 24, 1863, Johnny entered a Virginia City barbershop, asking for the works.

"I'm gunning for Peel," Johnny said, nonchalantly, "and I want to be a good-looking corpse if he gets me."

Peel heard about Johnny's plan as he nursed a drink in Pat Lynch's saloon. "Do unto others as they would do unto you, only do it first," he said, shrugging his shoulders. He enjoyed quoting a perverted scripture. "Tell him where he can find me."

With his cheeks shaved, his whiskers curled, and smelling of bay rum, Johnny stepped into the door of the saloon. "Any chiefs in here?" he asked.

"I suppose that remark is intended for me," Peel replied as he leaned against the bar, a shot glass in his hand. His soft voice was always well modulated. Some rumors said he had studied at Harvard. "Let's step outside and settle it."

"Sure thing," Johnny said as he turned back to the door.

Johnny reached the middle of C Street and turned in the bright sunshine to face the saloon, where Peel waited calmly in the shaded doorway. He would never fight an unarmed man or ambush an armed one; some things were just not done by gentlemen. He let Johnny go for his gun and fire first as Peel carefully aimed his pistol. Johnny's shot went wild, and Peel put a hole of death in Johnny's forehead.

"I guess that's what he wanted," Peel said softly, a touch of sorrow in his voice.

Langford Peel enjoyed great respect for his physical strength, his tall, slender, well-muscled body, his undoubted bravery, and—for much of the time—his great kindness. He began no quarrels, but he accepted no insults. He believed in an eye for an eye, and he could shoot accurately. God help the other man if he started something he could not finish.

"I'm very sorry," Peel said, almost in tears as he rejoined his friends in Lynch's saloon. "That poor fellow knew no more about handling a gun than an infant. But what could I do? If I had let him keep shooting, it could be me lying out there. I almost wish it was. Such a baby about guns."

"George," he called to the bartender, "run up to the mortuary and tell Brown to come down here and fix El Dorado up. Spare no expense. I'll pay for everything."

El Dorado Johnny made a fine-looking corpse. With his hair combed, his whiskers curled, and his clothing pressed, he lay in the saloon from Friday to Sunday. Seven bartenders kept busy making drinks for the thirsty horde that paid their respects to the brave but unskilled man lying peacefully in the magnificent, upholstered, silver-mounted casket, all paid for by Langford Peel.

The Sunday funeral procession to the cemetery was one of the largest that had been seen on the Comstock. A dark piece of sable hung on every saloon door. A shroud of crepe stretched over every gambling table. Even the mirrors were veiled in black. Much of the community grieved.

Pete Larkin, who later was hanged for murder, was master of ceremonies at the grave. Johnny was consigned to his last resting place, and the band struck up "When Johnny Comes Marching Home Again" as it marched back to Virginia City.

Peel was not punished for the killing, not even arrested. The law-abiding community felt relief that he was cleaning house of riffraff, and no policeman was anxious to meddle with the new chief of the Comstock.

But one day, Peel's conduct created a unanimous demand for his arrest, which was accomplished by the reluctant police assisted by a posse of outraged citizens. Justice of the Peace Davenport sentenced him to a $150 fine or twenty days in jail.

"I haven't any money, your honor," Peel said. "But if you'll release me on my own recognizance, I'll get it and settle up."

The judge, a mild man with a long beard of which he was very proud, consented. About a half hour later, Peel, his eyes sparkling, returned and walked up to the judge on his bench.

"Judge," he said very politely," I've come to settle that fine."

"Very good of you, Mister Peel," the judge said, stroking his magnificent beard and marveling at the subdued manner of the outlaw.

Then, Peel suddenly grabbed the judge's whiskers, wrapped them around both hands, and pounded his head against the wall until he was almost dead. The half dozen officers in the room stood quietly, looking at the butt of Peel's gun with respect. When Peel had "wooled" the judge's head to his satisfaction, he walked calmly out of the courtroom. The judge went on with his judicial business, considering the fine settled.

Although Peel eventually sent five challengers to new graves in Virginia City, he found life boring on the Comstock. In the winter of 1867, still a suave gentleman who dressed neatly and spoke softly, he moved to Belmont, Nevada, where he was employed by the owner of the Hornet Mine to recover possession from claim jumpers. Offered $500 for the successful recovery, Peel also insisted that he be appointed superintendent of the mine. He declined assistance, saying he would work alone.

With his written appointment in his hand, Peel strolled up to the mine entrance where the guard for the claim jumpers challenged him.

"I'm hired to take Dan Barlow's place on the shift," Peel responded casually. "I'm just going in to see the boss."

The guard let him go. When he reached the end of the tunnel, Peel put his back against a wall and called out to the miners, "Hold on, boys. I got something to read to you."

When he finished reading the appointment, he added pleasantly, "Now those of you that want to work for the Hornet Company can go to the office at any time this week and sign up. I'll let you know if we need you. In the meantime, you can all hold up your hands. Bill Mullen, don't reach for your gun unless you're looking for a coroner's inquest. My name is Farmer Peel and I'm going to count to twenty. When I get there, I'll start shooting at any man left in the mine. One, two, three—"

Long before he reached twenty, the mine was empty of claim jumpers and the rightful owners in possession.

While he was in Belmont, Peel met and became friends with Johnny Bull, another Englishman. He and Bull decided to try their luck in Montana. There Peel played his beloved faro while Bull, backed by Peel, tried mining in Last Chance Gulch in Helena.

Peel prospered better than Bull because Peel sometimes made up his own rules. Once, a young tenderfoot observing a game said to his older friend, "That faro dealer isn't on to his game. The man with the blonde beard has had three splits turned on to him and the dealer didn't collect on one. I thought you told me that two cards showing the same was a split and the dealer took half the bet."

"It is, but not so loud. That's Farmer Peel." Peel's customary nickname was a misspelling of his middle name, Farner. He had nothing to do with farming.

"Who's he?" the tenderfoot asked. "He don't look like a farmer."

"He's a desperado from the Comstock and he makes his own rules. Says a split is a standoff and won't let the dealer collect."

"What would happen if a dealer tried?"

"Don't know. No one's tried."

In July 1868 Johnny Bull showed up with such poor samples of ore that Peel accused his partner of double-crossing him. He even drew his gun in his rage.

"I'm not heeled," Bull said.

"Then go heel yourself," replied Peel, slapping Bull's face.

"I'll be back, Peel."

"Come afighting."

Peel was still known for never shooting an unarmed man or one unwilling to fight. If Bull had cooled off, nothing more would have happened. But he armed himself and returned.

This Johnny was unlike the brave, but naive El Dorado Johnny who let Peel shoot him from a shaded doorway after he had drawn and fired.

Peel's wooden gravestone marker

Montana Historical Society, Helena

Next to the saloon, where Peel was nursing his wrath with whiskey when Johnny Bull returned, was a store with a pile of large boxes in front. Bull hid behind these until Peel walked out of the saloon. Then he fired from ambush, without warning.

Peel had often bragged that someone might finally get him, but he would also get his assailant before he dropped himself. He never had a chance to prove that. When Johnny Bull's first shot dropped Peel, he leaped from his ambush and pumped three more shots into the prostrate body of his recent friend and partner.

The jury disagreed at Bull's murder trial. He skipped town right after, so there was no second trial.

A friend erected this monument at Peel's grave:

SACRED

to the

MEMORY

of

LANGFORD PEEL . . .

AGED

36 YEARS

IN LIFE BELOVED BY HIS FRIENDS

AND RESPECTED BY HIS

ENEMIES

VENGEANCE IS MINE

SAYETH THE LORD

I KNOW THAT MY REDEEMER

LIVETH

ERECTED BY A FRIEND

When the Pioneer Cemetery was moved to make way for Helena High School, the Montana Historical Society took possession of the wooden monument. The words, "I Know that my Redeemer Liveth" reflected Peel's view that anyone who finally killed him would, in turn, be killed by another who sought to be chief of the Comstock. The anonymous friend well expressed Peel's pleasure in perverting scripture.

Peel's redeemer never came. In 1929 Johnny Bull died a natural death in Vancouver, British Columbia. He was 93.

John Richard "Rattlesnake Dick"
——— Darling ———
The Perils of Rattlesnake Dick

John Richard Darling took the name Rattlesnake Dick, apparently after the more famous outlaw of the same name in California. He started out with petty crimes and drunkenness but was twice sentenced to prison. He could hold his own in the epic of Nevada outlawry, but his life was more tragic than violent.

In late summer 1863 Dick woke up one morning and discovered that he had enlisted in Company D of the First Battalion, Nevada Territorial Volunteers, Captain Baldwin commanding. With the regular soldiers transferred east for the Civil War, volunteer units had difficulty maintaining strength for protection against Indians. Company D did most of its recruiting in Virginia City, Gold Hill, and Dayton saloons.

Surprisingly, when Dick got over his hangover, he felt pride in being a soldier. He ran to tell joyous news to the woman who claimed to be his wife. She thought him an idiot and refused to live at Fort Churchill, his new duty post. For this ingratitude, Dick beat her up, and she decided to stay at a ranch 3 miles from the fort.

Before long, Dick began thinking seriously about his marital rights. On Saturday, September 12, 1863, he rode out to his beloved's new home, anxious to reestablish a more intimate relationship. But Monday's *Virginia Evening Bulletin* reported: "A gentlemen just in from the fort informs us that on Saturday the notorious Rattlesnake Dick was shot by his wife, the ball passing through his body and falling to the ground."

Virginia City Saloon
Nevada Historical Society, Reno

The next day's newspaper had more—and more accurate—details. When Dick arrived for his visit, his wife had met him with a double-barreled shotgun and "both barrels took effect in his left chest, seriously if not mortally wounding him."

But Dick survived his wifely welcome. He walked out to the road in front of the ranch, where Captain Baldwin picked him up and returned him to the fort. His nameless wife, now disillusioned with matrimony, disappeared from history. When Dick's enlistment ended in spring 1866, he turned to crime for a living, beginning with a nonviolent variety.

We don't know why Dick was over at Austin, but on the stage back to his Virginia City home, he met a young lady from Austin whose husband had sent her on a vacation to the States. Dick stole her watch and money, and when he reached Virginia City, his spending spree included many of the Comstock saloons. Pawning the watch financed his drinking as well as the purchase of companionship from one Bertha, whom he met in a saloon.

But when they reached Bertha's upstairs room, Dick passed out just outside her door. She had the bartender call the police, who arrested Dick, perhaps for obstructing traffic. Released the next morning, Dick returned to the saloon with a hangover and a club. He sneaked up behind the bartender, knocked him senseless, and then rushed upstairs to even his score with Bertha.

Bertha wasn't home, so Dick sat down to wait. He whiled the time away by sampling her stock of refreshments, and Bertha returned to find him passed out again. Dick was arrested and taken back to jail, but the bartender had to admit that he hadn't seen who hit him, so Dick was released on bail.

Rattlesnake Dick charged back to Bertha's crib, but she convinced him that they had no future. She, too, disappeared from history.

The proceeds of Dick's petty theft lasted only ten days. Then, it would appear that he turned to violent crime. The Virginia City newspaper for the last few days in May reported that Dick and a companion named M.M. Woods had broken into a locked saloon on Virginia City's main street and nearly beaten a customer, Patrick McCauley, to death. Jessie Case, the young woman who kept the saloon, had to run an errand so she had locked up, telling McCauley, the only customer, that she'd be back shortly.

Jessie returned to find the back door broken open, blood all over the floor, and McCauley unconscious and beaten so badly he was hardly recognizable. Blood covered his face, and broken glass littered the floor. When he recovered enough to talk, McCauley said he worked on a ranch on the Carson River, about 25 miles away, and that he had been robbed of $300. He had no idea how his assailant or assailants got in and attacked him. The May 26 *Territorial Enterprise* "earnestly hoped that the police could obtain some kind of clue leading to the arrest and conviction of the scoundrels concerned in this high-handed piece of villainy."

Police Captain George Downey learned that Dick had been living across the street at the Occidental Hotel for four or five days and had suddenly disappeared. Before the disappearance he had been hanging out at the saloon in question. The police found McCauley's wallet in Dick's room, and the hotel proprietor said Dick had told her that he was going to nearby Washoe Valley to visit his father. Downey tracked his man to Ophir in Washoe Valley, where he was hiding out in an old house, and there made the arrest on the day following the crime.

The newspaper reported that McCauley eventually identified Dick as one of the two men he saw in the bar, although he did not know which one had struck him from behind. The police never found Woods. Dick claimed that Woods told him that he had won $100 from McCauley and that McCauley pulled a knife on him. Then, Woods said that he hit McCauley with a bottle and left the saloon, telling Dick that he was leaving the state. Dick even claimed that he was not in the saloon when Woods did the crime. The judge turned a deaf ear to those statements.

So did the jury. After their guilty verdict, Judge Richard Rising sentenced Dick to fourteen years in prison at hard labor. But the transcript of the testimony before the magistrate, upon which Dick was held in custody until he went to trial, throws grave doubt on the trial jury's quick verdict, the judge's heavy sentence, and the newspaper's presentation of the facts.

Victim McCauley testified before the magistrate that he entered the saloon on Friday, May 25, between nine and ten o'clock. He saw two men there. One asked him to play cards, and McCauley said he did not have time. When he turned around to leave, he was struck on the back of the head. He had about $160 in gold and silver, and when he came to he only had $28 in loose coins.

McCauley identified Dick as one of the men in the saloon, but could not say which of the two hit him as his back was turned. He was sure that Dick was not the one who asked him to play cards. McCauley was out in the street when he came to. He said he had entered the saloon to light his pipe, and he was there only two or three minutes.

On cross-examination, McCauley said there was no one behind the bar when he entered. He had seen Dick in the saloon before and had bought him a drink. At that time, Dick was with the same man that he saw there when he was attacked.

Jessie Case testified that she saw McCauley in her saloon between ten and eleven o'clock. She served him a drink, and he drank with Dick, a frequent customer, and another man whom she did not know. After five or ten minutes, the three men left and she closed and locked the saloon, putting the front door key in her pocket and the rear door key in her money drawer. She returned in about an hour and the front door was still locked, but the back door was ajar. She saw blood in the back room.

Constable Augustus Ash testified that he saw McCauley between ten and eleven o'clock washing himself behind Ash's office. Then Ash went to Jessie's saloon, where he found the front door unlocked and a broken bottle and blood in the back room. He and Police Chief Downey went to Ophir and arrested Dick, who was lying on a bed with his boots on.

Dick's lawyer did not let him testify. Five years would pass before his version reached the authorities. The action taken then suggests that Dick may have been innocent of this crime and railroaded into prison.

Dick's prison term began June 30, 1866. Five years later, Richard Rising, the trial judge, wrote Nevada Lieutenant Governor Frank Denver, saying he thought five years was a sufficient sentence, and he would concur in Rattlesnake Dick's application for a pardon. He said his very stiff sentence reflected the community's feeling at the time about violent crime.

"I would say that at the time of his sentence many outrages and crimes had been and were constantly being committed in this city, and to endeavor to create a terror upon evil doers," Rising wrote. "I imposed upon those convicted very severe punishments."

Dick's fourteen years was the longest sentence Judge Rising had ever given for robbery and assault. Two months later, the governor responded with a pardon for Dick.

But we have more than the trial judge's letter of regret. Dick's statement of facts surrounding the conviction, filed in his application for pardon, states that on Friday, May 25, 1866, he had been in Jessie Case's saloon with McCauley and M.M. Woods. Woods had brought him a note from a sick woman in Ophir saying she wanted to see him. He left immediately, and McCauley and Woods started playing cards. He reached Ophir about 3:00 P.M. and stayed all night with a man named Kelley who kept a saloon there.

While Dick was there, Woods arrived, saying he'd had trouble with McCauley about the card game. Woods said that McCauley threw a knife at him, and then he struck McCauley on the head with a bottle and left the saloon.

"It's too hot for me here," Woods had said, and he left town.

The next morning Constable Ash and Police Chief Downey arrested Dick. Downey told him that if he could find Woods, he would not want Dick. But Downey "was determined if he could not find Woods to convict me of the charge," Dick said in a statement.

Dick's statement also charged McCauley with later robbing another man and with betraying his own brother into the California State Prison. He said another of McCauley's brothers was hanged.

Finally, Dick denied having anything to do with the robbery of McCauley. He also mentioned that he had once been a soldier.

Dick's petition for a pardon had drawn the written support of the committing magistrate, the district attorney, the constable and the police chief who arrested him, the United States Marshal, and two of the trial jurors.

Rattlesnake Dick got his pardon in 1871, but his perils continued.

Just over a year later, in November 1872, Dick was back in prison for robbing Colonel M.N. Stone on the highway below Silver City, a few miles from Virginia City. Colonel Stone was a lawyer, and in late October he was making frequent political speeches for his party. On the evening of October 24, while traveling in a buggy after making a speech, he was held up by two masked men wearing linen dusters.

The taller of the two men resembled Rattlesnake Dick in appearance. Apparently the shorter man did all the talking. The shorter man removed Stone's purse and watch from his pocket. The purse contained $55. Then he told Stone to get back in the buggy and "drive like hell," which Stone did.

The next morning Stone and Deputy Sheriff B.P. Lackey went to the holdup scene. They followed the boot tracks of the robbers to a fresh buggy track out in the sagebrush. The buggy had come from the direction of Carson City and returned in that direction.

"Probably rented there," Lackey said. "The town's full with the horse races going on."

The next day, Lackey and Stone learned that Rattlesnake Dick and one Edwin Booth had rented a buggy in Carson City the afternoon of the robbery, returning it the next day. They had also borrowed a couple of linen dusters to wear. The deputy and Stone went out to the races and saw Dick there. Later that afternoon, Stone and Dick had a conversation.

"How much would you pay if I found your watch for you?" Dick asked.

"A hundred dollars. How soon can you get it?"

"I'll meet you in an hour at Frisbie's Saloon. Bring the money."

But when Stone told Lackey and Sheriff Swift of this conversation, they insisted on arresting Dick immediately. Stone wanted to wait until Dick appeared with the watch, but Swift made the arrest anyway.

Stone went to the station after Dick was brought in, without the watch. Dick reminded him that he was to pay $100 for the watch.

"I meant I'd pay it if the watch was found with the men who robbed me," Stone said.

"If they'll release me, I'll find the robbers and the watch."

The sheriff left with Dick, and they returned in twenty minutes. This time Dick had the watch. Again Dick asked to be released, offering to find the robbers. The sheriff refused to release Dick and returned in about fifteen minutes with a William Chamberlin in custody. Apparently, Dick had given Sheriff Swift Chamberlin's name.

When Stone saw Chamberlin in the sheriff's office, he accused him of being one of the robbers. After initial denials, Chamberlin admitted leaving Carson City with Dick in a rented buggy.

All three suspects were charged with the robbery, and Will Campbell appeared as attorney to represent Booth. Before the trial began, the district attorney dismissed the charges against Booth, probably on condition that he testify against the other two. Trial Judge Seawall then appointed Campbell to represent Dick and Chamberlin. Campbell protested the violation of ethical rules, pointing out that he could not represent men who had a conflict of interest with each other and with his former client. Furthermore, he argued, he could not be expected to cross-examine Booth about matters told him by Booth in confidence. Judge Seawall insisted that he defend Dick and Chamberlin.

A witness testified at the trial that he had seen three men in a buggy going toward Carson City from Silver City on the night of the 24th. It stopped in front of a saloon, and two men went inside while a third stayed in the buggy. He also testified that Dick had admitted to him that he was one of the two men who went in for drinks and brought out a drink for the man in the buggy. In the preliminary examination before trial, Chamberlin had admitted that he, Dick, and Booth were the three men in the buggy at that time.

Dick testified in his own defense. He said Chamberlin had robbed Stone, and that he knew where the victim's watch was because he had seen the chain protruding from under the pillow where it was hidden. He did not know who put it there. He denied doing it himself.

After two days of testimony, the jury found both Dick and Chamberlin guilty. The judge sentenced each to ten years in prison. Considering himself a silent observer of Chamberlin's robbery, Dick probably shook his head in confusion. Perhaps he looked at Campbell, shaking his head at the impossible situation his attorney had been forced into.

Dick served eight years of the sentence without difficulty, although he once served a month in the dungeon for possession of a large knife. But in July 1880 he killed Chamberlin by striking him over the head with a pick. Dick, a trusty at the time, was working alone with Chamberlin in the prison quarry. Dick claimed that Chamberlin attacked him with a pick handle, and he acted in self-defense. The prison authorities must have believed Dick because he was not prosecuted for the killing or even disciplined for it.

Dick was released in 1881, at the conclusion of his ten-year sentence. He appeared briefly in Virginia City and then disappeared.

In addition to seeking a new environment away from old acquaintances and suspicious police, Dick tried honest employment. He got hired as a brakeman on the Carson and Colorado Railroad. This narrow gauge line connected with the Virginia and Truckee at Mound House to run southerly through Lyon and Esmeralda Counties, terminating in Inyo County, California, after a distance of 293 miles.

Dick made his new home in Hawthorne, Nevada, at about the mid-point of his employer's line. But unfortunately, his new job had not changed enough of Dick's customary behavior. In August 1883 Dick got into a saloon argument with James Warren, an ex-convict better known as Jimmy Fresh. Each accused the other of stealing money from a prostitute.

While on his way to work the next morning, Dick met Warren on the street. Warren drew his pistol saying, "You'll not threaten my life again," and shot Dick in the face. He pumped two more bullets into Dick's dead body after it fell.

The newspaper account of Dick's final affray said he was forty-three and a native of Kentucky. After service in the War against Mexico [impossible unless he was a seven-year-old drummer boy], he had moved to Salt Lake City and lived with the Mormons. He married but deserted his wife to come to the Comstock after the silver discovery of 1859.

"He had been in numerous deadly affrays," the newspaper reported, "and was regarded as a desperate character. Darling's life was an eventful one, and if written up would furnish material for a first-class dime novel."

Bravery at
──»─•─«──Bullion Bend──»─•─«──

Bullion Bend, about 14 miles east of Placerville, California, got its name on June 30, 1864, when supporters of the Confederacy robbed two stages that left Nevada that morning. The robbery and the gunfights that followed have been called the farthest west battle of the Civil War. The two stages traveled together, leaving Virginia City at five o'clock in the morning and due in Placerville at ten that evening. Their twenty-eight passengers were divided evenly between the first coach, driven by Frank Blair, and the rear one with Charley Watson on the reins. Charley assigned seven riders to the inside and seven on top. One of his passengers, a plucky sixteen-year-old girl whose name we don't know, wore a Garibaldi jacket with big jet-black buttons. She caught Charley's eye, and he assigned her the seat of honor beside him.

After a brief stop at Gold Hill, the stages headed west through Carson City, up the mountain to Friday's Station at Lake Bigler (now Tahoe) and over Johnson Pass, where the men passengers had to get out and push. As the day wore on, passing through tall sugar pine and majestic fir, the passengers grew tired. When they reached the south fork of the American River, the young girl moved inside to get some sleep.

Shortly before ten, as the lead coach slowed to make a sharp turn in a narrow canyon, Frank Blair looked up to see six hooded men holding torches and revolvers. He reined in, and two men jumped aboard and threw down the strong box.

"Gentlemen," their leader announced, "I will tell you who we are."

The robbers were Ingraham's Partisan Rangers, and Rufus Henry Ingraham, a tall, slender, rawboned man, spoke with confidence. A veteran of service with Quantrill's Raiders, including the raid on Lawrence,

Stagecoach descending the mountain
Nevada Historical Society, Reno

Kansas, where every man in town was killed, Ingraham was well educated and well mannered. He had chosen Tom Poole, a burly Kentuckian who had been undersheriff of Monterey County, California, as his lieutenant. The others were George Baker, John Bouldware, John Clendenning, and Al Glasby, the youngest at nineteen.

"We are not robbers," Ingraham said, "but a company of Confederate soldiers. Now, don't do anything foolish. We don't want anything of you passengers; just Wells Fargo's treasure to assist us in recruiting for the Confederacy." The robbery required only a few minutes, and the robbers waived Blair's stage on as the second one rumbled up.

A passenger in the front stage, Virginia City police officer McDougall, foolishly fired his revolver at the robbers, as his coach moved away. He didn't hit anyone, but he made some of the robbers mad. The second coach's passengers heard one robber say, "Now we ought to shoot the whole damn bunch."

Charley Watson, reining up his team, shouted to the robbers, "Now those shots didn't come from any of us, so don't take it out on this stage." He turned toward his passengers and continued. "Them shots spooked my horses, and we're setting on a damn narrow road some distance above the bottom of the ravine. Any more shooting and we're likely to be smashed to smithereens. You hear?"

Ingraham gave the same greeting to Watson's passengers about recruiting for the Confederacy, and Watson handed down two sacks of bullion. But the robbers, perhaps thinking they didn't get as much as expected from the first stage, looked in the boot and found another bag of bullion and a bag of express freight that looked heavy enough to be promising.

The second stage carried four women besides the young girl, who by now was wide awake. While the robbers completed their job, the girl engaged them in conversation.

"You men say you are soldiers," the girl said. "Do you have a flag?"

"Yes ma'am."

"Could I see it?"

"It's not convenient right now. We're too busy."

The man's pistol came near the girl's face. She waved it away, her curiosity changed to a calm, steely coolness.

"Could you please lower that, sir? It might go off accidentally, you know."

"I'm sorry ma'am. We're all southern gentlemen. We would rather protect young ladies than injure them." He lowered the pistol.

"Are you going to take all four bags?"

"Yes, ma'am," another voice answered.

"How can you carry it all away?"

"We all got horses."

"You say you're recruiting for the South?"

"Yes ma'am."

"How can you spend bullion?"

"We'll figure out a way."

"What will you buy with it?"

"Things we need for the Confederacy." By now, three or four of the robbers had been drawn into answering the girl's questions.

After the robbers had secured their bullion and the freight bag, they asked if the passengers wanted to contribute to the Southern cause.

"Will you take greenbacks?" the girl asked.

"We don't want no greenbacks. We got no use for that currency."

"Well I do have some five-cent postal currency in my pocket, but I won't give it up without a fight." The girl pressed her lips together, shaking her head firmly.

"We don't fight young ladies."

Ingraham handed Charley Watson a handwritten note reading: "This is to certify that I have received from Wells, Fargo and Co. the sum of $_____cash, for the purpose of outfitting recruits enlisted in California for the Confederate States' Army. R. Henry Ingraham, Captain, Commanding Co., C.S.A."

He didn't fill in the blank.

After the robbers had ridden off, one of the men passengers asked the girl, "Why did you ask so many questions?"

"We couldn't see their faces for the hoods," she replied. "I thought we should hear their voices. It might help identify them if they're caught."

A man passenger in Watson's stage, interviewed by the *Sacramento Daily Union*, complimented the girl for her grit. He said she was much more self-possessed than any of the others. "If I knew her name," he added, "I would give it to Chief Burke with a recommendation that she be employed on detective duty."

During the next day or two, reports of the amount of coin and bullion taken in the robbery varied from $5,000 to $40,000. The newspaper initially reported that twelve silver bricks and some gold coin had been taken. They placed the value at over $40,000. Wells Fargo claimed that the loss did not exceed $3,000. The first robbers captured contributed to the discrepancy by saying that they were interested only in robbery, not in Confederate recruiting, and claiming that their leader had taken $20,000 with him when they separated.

A close reading of the Virginia City newspapers shows that Wells Fargo was correct on the amount, and that the robbers picked the wrong day's stages to rob. The June 29 *Gold Hill Daily News* reported that three bricks of bullion from the Gem mine, worth $1,200, had been delivered to the stage to be shipped. That would, of course, have gone out early the next day on the stages the robbers attacked. But the same newspaper reported that the stages that day had carried thirty-two bars of bullion and one more package, with an assayed value of almost $60,000. So the robbers were a day late and over $50,000 short!

The robbed coaches reached Placerville after midnight, and the drivers notified the sheriff. He dispatched Deputy Joe Staples and Constables John Van Eaton and George Ranney south toward Diamond Springs, while he led a posse of citizens back to the scene of the robbery. At dawn, the deputy and the constables found tracks of six riders heading south toward the Somerset House. Van Eaton had been wounded in a shootout a few weeks earlier, and was not fully recovered, so he rode back to advise the sheriff. Staples and Ranney continued to follow the tracks.

Meanwhile, when the robbers reached the Somerset House they saw Maria Reynolds, a young divorcee who was staying with Mrs. Davis, the proprietor. Captain Ingraham told her that he and his men would like breakfast, and Maria went to waken Mrs. Davis. While the ladies cooked breakfast, Ingraham, Poole, and Glasby lay down for a nap, and the other men went into the woods for some target practice.

Then Staples and Ranney rode up. When Staples went into the kitchen to ask if any men had recently arrived, he saw a loaded shotgun on the porch. The women nodded silently and pointed to show that the men were there. Staples went back to pick up the shotgun, while Ranney barged into the robbers' room, saying, "Good morning, have you seen any men riding by during the night?" He heard a few gruff noes and backed out quickly to see Staples cocking the shotgun.

"They're inside," Ranney told Staples. "Let's wait and make a plan."

But Staples had had his courage questioned in the earlier shootout where Van Eaton was wounded, and he didn't want to wait. He bolted through the door, shotgun in hand, and ordered all present to throw up their hands. Instead, they met him with a fusillade of bullets, and Staples was dead by the time he slumped to the floor. He did have time to fire the shotgun and wound Thomas Poole.

The other robbers ran outside, saw Ranney, and shot him as he tried to reach his horse. As they moved in for the kill, Mrs. Reynolds shielded Ranney's body with hers, shaming the gunmen for cowardly trying to kill a wounded man who was obviously going to die anyway. She convinced them, and they mounted their horses and rode away.

Mrs. Reynolds's courage probably saved Ranney's life, as he was seriously, but not mortally, wounded.

Meanwhile, when the sheriff got to Bullion Bend, he arrested two men at nearby Thirteen-Mile-House on the mistaken identification of Frank Blair, the driver of the first coach. While the sheriff had the two men in custody, Van Eaton arrived with the news that Staples and Ranney were following the tracks of six men. The sheriff did not think they could be the robbers because he thought at that time that he had two of the robbers under arrest. He was criticized for being slow to follow what turned out to be the correct trail.

While Deputy Joe Staples was being buried in Placerville, Tom Poole, the man he had wounded, was arrested. Poole mumbled through his bandages that he had recently been undersheriff of Monterey

County and he knew nothing about the robbery. Charley Watson was present, and he identified the voice, glad that a brave young girl had kept Poole and others talking.

Eventually the two men initially arrested were released. Perhaps they would have never been arrested, and the sheriff would not have been delayed in pursuit, if Frank Blair, the driver of the leading stage, had heard more talk from the robbers.

Sheriff Rogers of Calaveras County took up the robbers' trail and lost it near West Point. There, the robbers had seen a gang of horse thieves. Mistaking them for a posse, the robbers panicked, abandoned their camp—supplies, horses, and all—and fled on foot across the San Joaquin Valley. They stole more horses near Livermore Pass and reached San Jose on July 10. After several days hiding out with a Mr. Hill, their host had second thoughts and got word to Santa Clara County Sheriff Adams about the men.

On July 15 Adams and nine deputies surrounded Hill's house, and demanded the robbers surrender. A gunfight followed in which several officers were wounded and two robbers, Bouldware and Clendenning, killed. Young Alban Glasby surrendered. When questioned, Glasby referred to the young girl they had talked to as "a brick," a term in those days for a bar of bullion, obviously used by Glasby in admiration for the girl's courage.

Glasby, from Missouri, claimed that he was operating under authority of the Confederate government and wanted prisoner-of-war status, which was denied. Then he agreed to testify in return for a dismissal of his charges. He related the details of the robbery and the killing of Staples and testified in the trials that lasted over the next two years. Poole was hanged. Ingraham and Baker were never found.

John Moriarty

A Young Irishman in the Mines

John Moriarty, born in Caharciveen, Kerry County, Ireland, about 1844, showed up at a dance in the Niagara Dance Hall on B Street in Virginia City, Nevada, in November 1868. Between dances he walked to the adjoining saloon and ordered a glass of wine. The bartender poured whiskey instead.

"I asked for wine," Moriarty objected.

The bartender curled his lip and sneered, "Whiskey is good enough for the likes of you."

The Irishman squared off as though to punch the bartender when John O'Toole grabbed his arm, saying, "Watch it, my lad, or you'll be feeling the might of Irish knuckles."

Moriarty, as Irish as O'Toole, whipped out his revolver, turned to put his back to the wall, and covered O'Toole as well as the rest of the men crowding into the room. The room hushed as he backed slowly out a side door, his revolver held steady against the threatening crowd. Then the short-tempered man made his big mistake.

Moriarty walked around to the front door of the saloon, the upper half of which was glass. He saw O'Toole standing at the bar, his back toward the door. Taking careful aim, he shot and killed O'Toole. Later he would claim that O'Toole had thrown a glass at him, as though that would excuse the cold-blooded killing. Moriarty left town in a hurry, changed his name to Morgan Courtney, and showed up two years later at Pioche, the center of mining in southeastern Nevada.

He said he had come from Salt Lake City, although he may have

Pioche mining camp
Nevada Historical Society, Reno

spent some time in Montana after fleeing from Nevada. He gave the appearance of a quiet, reserved man, but he had only three items of luggage when he got off the stage in Pioche—a Henry rifle, a six-shooter, and a small satchel.

Many considered Pioche the toughest mining town in the West. Historians count forty killings between 1870 and 1875, with only two men punished. The official report of the Nevada commissioner of mining in 1872 said that two classes of people struck it rich in Pioche: lawyers hired to maintain titles of mining claims and scoundrels hired to maintain their possession.

The geography and geology of Pioche contributed to its violence. All the early, rich strikes were made in claims located in a small area on Treasure Hill, a low but sometimes steep mountain. The claims overlapped, and the county had not established a legal system for unraveling ownership entanglements, leaving the problem to the miners themselves.

In fact the language in the Federal Mining Law of 1872, still effective today, which defines the right to follow mineral veins through claims staked by others, resulted directly from the Pioche problem. That law was largely written by Nevada's first United States senator, William Stewart, and he knew the facts of the problem. But the owners at the time the problem arose learned quickly to hire gunmen to keep other gunmen from jumping their claims. When Courtney learned that legitimate miners hired outlaws to protect their claims from others, he knew he had found a home.

Brothers Tom and Frank Newland had a claim on the steep hillside above the Washington & Creole, the richest mine in town. They got permission to tunnel through the Washington & Creole to reach a deeply buried vein on their claim. While they were tunneling, they struck a rich vein in the Washington & Creole, and got permission from the owners to mine that ore for thirty days.

The thirty days expired and the Newland Brothers resumed their tunneling, but the temptation to take out more ore from the fabulous discovery was too much, even for them. Under cover of darkness they built a log fort at the entrance to their tunnel, hired gunmen to jump the Washington & Creole, and stocked the fort with ammunition and supplies for a siege. They continued mining the Washington & Creole, keeping the rightful owners away at gunpoint.

At this stage Morgan Courtney entered the melodrama. He hired three young gunmen, Michael Casey, Barney Flood, and William Bethards, and contracted with the Washington & Creole to drive the Newland crowd off, receiving permission to mine the newly discovered vein themselves for thirty days after they had chased off the Newland men.

Courtney studied the fort carefully and decided against a direct assault. He would rely on two prominent vices well known in the mines—dishonesty and intemperance.

The Newland gunmen must have thought that the shipment of whiskey delivered to their fort came by mistake. The brothers and their henchmen wondered how those strangers delivering the goods could believe that the address they sought was up on the side of the mountain. But they winked, nudged each other, and accepted delivery. Besides, the night wind on November 8, 1870, was cold, and the men, tired of their long vigil, gleefully opened the bottles to celebrate their victory over the rightful owners of the vein. At about three in the morning, when even the night watch had had its fill, Courtney's gang charged down the mountain, battle cries on their lips and smoking revolvers in their hands.

One would call it a humane attack by Pioche standards; only one defender was killed and the rest ran away from their arms and ammunition. Morgan Courtney and his three men took over as kings of the hill—or at least of the fort that controlled access to the treasure.

Courtney and one of the Newlands were wounded, neither seriously. But a Newland man, W.G. Snell, lay dead. The county indicted Courtney, alone, for Snell's murder. Nothing came of the indictment. Lincoln County's incomplete court records show no trial, and the newspapers that would have covered it have been lost.

In the meantime the four men took about $60,000 worth of ore out of the Washington & Creole during their thirty-day "lease," selling the ore to its rightful owner. Michael Casey received nothing good from his share of the money. On the day it was delivered, he went to the bank to make his deposit and got in an argument with a Thomas Gorson about interest Casey owed him on a loan. They drew their guns, and Casey won the argument by better shooting. But three months later, when witness James Levy said Casey had fired first, Casey got the help of David Nagle and then unwisely threatened to make Levy eat his words. Although outnumbered two to one, Levy killed Casey.

William Bethards killed a man three years later and went to prison, where another inmate killed him.

This left Morgan Courtney and Barney Flood of the four who had attacked the fort. They were arrested the next February for the knife murder of Thomas Coleman in Pioche. Both men were fond of knives, but both were released for lack of evidence. Flood left Pioche after stabbing another man who did not die.

Courtney, the only one of the four gunmen left in Pioche, had become a hero in all the saloons. For once, he had won a fight on the side of perceived justice, if not on the side of law. Probably for the first time in his life, he had plenty of money to spend. And he spent it freely, mostly in gambling.

Courtney also developed a taste for fancy clothes. He prided himself on ordering suits of the finest black broadcloth and shirts of the purest white linen, all decorated with the most expensive looking jewelry. He also had his fingernails manicured, certainly unusual behavior in Pioche. A stranger in town might have thought Courtney owned the Washington & Creole. In fact its true owners were a strange pair. W.H. Raymond, with his hunched back, stood 5 feet tall. His partner John H. Ely was 6 feet, 3 inches tall. They both excelled in courage and cared little about their appearance. Their mine would eventually pay $13 million in dividends.

On June 8, 1872, in Caucey's Saloon on Pioche's steep main street, Courtney and John Sullivan had words about whether or not Sullivan had invited Courtney to drink with him. Courtney, disgusted with the trivial argument, left the saloon, but Sullivan followed. Courtney would claim at his trial that Sullivan tried to sell him some mining stock. When Courtney said no, Sullivan drew his knife and said, "You damned son of a bitch, I'll kill you yet."

Courtney drew his revolver and backed out of range of Sullivan's knife, saying, "Take that back or I'll kill you."

Sullivan didn't and Courtney did. He shot Sullivan from 30 feet away.

Courtney spent the rest of the summer in the Lincoln County jail. The prosecution took nine days for its case, and the district attorney took five hours for his summation to the jury in the crowded courtroom, so they must have really wanted Courtney off the street. But juries didn't take kindly to the language Sullivan had used, sometimes deciding that it gave the other combatant the right to shoot. The saloon crowd pulled for Courtney, and at about one o'clock on Sunday morning the jury returned a verdict of acquittal.

Courtney's joy was dampened when the Lincoln County sheriff, with an old warrant from Storey County for the killing of O'Toole four years before, promptly rearrested Courtney. Fearing vigilante action when the community learned of the acquittal, he had his prisoner on a stage for Virginia City before the day was over.

But Courtney's luck was still with him. Although the Virginia City killing had occurred in a crowded saloon, only one witness was known to be still alive, and he could not be brought to court. The charge was dismissed and Courtney returned to Pioche, where Sullivan's friends had already forgotten their anger at the verdict. For the first time in four years, Courtney did not feel a noose hanging over his head. He even got respectable, staking out a mining claim, which he called The Faro Bank.

In January 1873 Courtney and several partners—including the man who had killed Courtney's partner, Mike Casey, less than two years before—made arrangements to develop a mine. As the Irishman's business prospects improved, so did his love life. By then he was superintendent of the Kentucky Mine, and he had met and got involved with Georgianne "Georgie" Scyphers. Georgie worked in a brothel, but she knew how to hold her own with men. Once, when a man assaulted her in the brothel, she shot him with her pistol. Later, she killed a man for defaming her sister. She was just the woman for hair-triggered Morgan Courtney.

Apart from paying customers, the only other man in Georgie Scyphers's life was James McKinney. There was bad blood between

OUTLAW TALES OF NEVADA

McKinney and Courtney from the start. McKinney claimed that a few years before, his best friend was killed in Montana and he thought Courtney was the killer.

On a pleasant summer's evening in 1873, Courtney demanded that McKinney tell him the whereabouts of Georgie.

"I'm not keeping track of her," McKinney snorted.

But Georgie had claimed to others that she was the center of a love triangle, involving McKinney and Courtney. In fact, when she failed to meet McKinney in his room, as she had promised, McKinney said it was because she was afraid of Courtney.

"I'll wring your heart worse than you've ever wrung mine, before you'll ever lay with me again," McKinney told Georgie.

Georgie also swore that McKinney had often said he hated Courtney. "He said he hated him because other men feared him," she said.

On Friday, August 1, 1873, the night Georgie stood McKinney up, he armed himself and went looking for Courtney. He carried a double-action revolver—unusual at that time—that could be fired as fast as one could pull the trigger. The large weapon would not fit into McKinney's pocket. He thrust the barrel into the pocket and kept his right hand on the butt and his left curled over the cylinder to keep the gun from falling out. He searched up and down the narrow, steep streets for his rival, carefully looking both ways before crossing a side street.

He found Courtney coming out of the Mint Saloon walking, as he usually did, with his right hand in his coat pocket holding his own pistol. McKinney later claimed that Courtney was moving purposely toward him, when McKinney drew his weapon and said, "Courtney, I am here to fight." Then, according to McKinney, Courtney made a move to draw his gun and McKinney started pulling the trigger.

An eyewitness said that when McKinney fired the first shot, Courtney seemed to freeze as though unsure what to do. Then Courtney turned and ran, stooping forward as he dodged from side to side. Other witnesses agreed that Courtney froze at the first shot, as though surprised at someone standing up to him and uncertain how to handle it. As Courtney turned and ran, he seemed to be trying to draw his own revolver but was unable to get it out of his pocket.

McKinney followed, blasting away from a distance of 3 to 4 feet. In desperation Courtney ducked into a saloon and out again on a side street. Then Deputy Sheriff J.R. Hoge arrived. He grabbed McKinney and disarmed him. But McKinney had already emptied his fast-shooting revolver.

When the shooting stopped, Courtney staggered out of the steep side street with his revolver dangling from his left hand. By then Hoge was dragging McKinney to jail, followed by a threatening crowd. Some of the onlookers carried Courtney into a drug store and laid him carefully on the floor, where a doctor examined him. Five of McKinney's six shots had hit him, one from the front and four from the back. His immaculate linen coat, now smeared with spreading bloodstains, had even caught fire from the close-range shooting.

J.P. Kirby, a witness to the gun battle, said that one or two nights before the shooting he had overheard a conversation between Courtney and McKinney.

"You son of a bitch," Courtney said, "I thought I told you to leave this town, and you had better do it or I will kill you."

"Courtney, why do you follow me up?" McKinney had replied.

Kirby said he moved on and heard no more. Others corroborated that Courtney had complained about McKinney not leaving town.

While the crowd speculated about the reason behind the one-sided fight, the doctor told Courtney he could not live, and if he had anything to say he should say it quickly. Between heavily drawn gasps of breath and pausing now and then to gather his strength, Courtney slowly dictated a dying statement, which was written down by a newspaper reporter.

He said, "I think I am going to die. I was walking down the street and McKinney shot me in the back. I started to run in order to get in a place to defend myself but he shot so fast that I could not do anything but run. I did not shoot at McKenney at all. I did not get my pistol out until he fired six shots. Georgie Scyphers told me that Frank Cleveland gave McKinney a pistol yesterday."

Courtney's dying statement was interrupted once when a Catholic priest gave him the last rites. The torn piece of wrapping paper upon which the dying statement was written and witnessed remains in the present courthouse at Pioche. The man who had terrorized the town had nothing to say about the cold-blooded killings of Sullivan and O'Toole, nothing about the many unsolved murders where he was suspected, no regrets, no advice to friends about learning from his mistakes. There was not even a word for Georgie, just a recital of how he had been cut down in cold blood, as he had done others. Morgan Courtney died that night, aged twenty-nine.

The Pioche *Record* said, "Morgan Courtney, feared by some, detested by others, and respected by a few, was a desperate character. He had killed his man in Pioche some fourteen months ago, a murderer in the broadest acceptance of the term. We only refer to his tragic death as a verification of the prophecy that those who slay by the sword shall by the sword be slain."

The publisher of the newspaper ordered the volunteer fire company he commanded to turn out in full uniform for the funeral of their fallen comrade, Morgan Courtney.

The funeral procession, led by a Catholic priest and by Courtney's cousin, William J. Kelly, both in a buggy, followed by a brass band, the volunteer fire company, and over 300 citizens, moved to Boot Hill to bury Courtney.

The law handled McKinney's case. In this he was lucky, as plans had been made to storm the jail and accomplish justice with a rope. The trial started September 10 and lasted ten days. It took the jury three minutes to acquit him.

The Pioche *Record* on August 8 reported that within the previous thirty days, ten pistol shots and thirteen knife wounds had been inflicted by three Pioche citizens on their victims. The grisly accounting of violent bodily punctures included, besides McKinney's five shots into Courtney, one Huntington who inflicted five gunshot wounds on four men, one mortally, and a Ferguson who had stabbed his victim thirteen times, also mortally. Altogether, Pioche saw five homicides in the four months leading up to the McKinney trial.

Although his funeral procession to Boot Hill was impressive, Irishman John Moriarty is buried in an unmarked grave. The Boot Hill part of the Pioche Cemetery lies along its south border. Some of the thirty-seven mounds have old boots lying on them, one has an old hat, and some have nothing. None of them is identified. No one knows which one contains the bones of John Moriarty.

Train of Destiny

Shortly after midnight on November 5, 1870, Central Pacific No. 1, an eastbound express with a combination express-baggage car, day coach, and sleeper, slowed for the track siding that served the lumber mill at Verdi, Nevada. Conductor Frank Mitchell and Wells Fargo Guard Frank Marshall knew that the train carried $41,800 in $20 gold coins for payrolls at Comstock mines and $8,800 in silver bars for deposit in Nevada banks. They did not know that history would mark that day with the first train robbery west of the Rocky Mountains. And if someone had suggested that the second train robbery in the West would happen to the same train—even before it left Nevada—and that the robberies were completely coincidental, anyone would have scoffed.

As the train eased past the lumber mill, six men wearing black masks and linen dusters dashed out into the bright moonlight and jumped aboard, two on the engine and four at the rear. When Conductor Mitchell saw handguns instead of tickets, he thought the men were stealing rides. But he didn't argue when they said, "Be quiet and you won't get hurt." When the train came to a brief stop and two men forced the brakeman forward to unhook the express-baggage car from the passenger cars, Mitchell knew that his train was being robbed. He watched ruefully as the last two robbers ran forward and the business half of the train, with its valuable cargo, receded in the distance.

Marshall, alone in the express car with the gold and silver, expected a stop at Reno to deliver the payroll. But when the engine stopped at an abandoned stone quarry near Lawton's Springs, about halfway between Reno and Verdi, he heard a knock on the door.

"Who's there?" Marshall asked.

"It's Small. Open up."

Verdi train robbery, November 5, 1870
Nevada Historical Society, Reno

Marshall opened the door and saw six masked men holding guns on his engineer. The outlaws broke the strongbox open and grabbed over $40,000 in gold coin. They left only the silver bars—too heavy to carry—and bank currency notes—too dangerous to spend.

A.J. "Big Jack" Davis, an experienced stage robber, led the robbers. They included John Squires, also a veteran stage robber; E.B. Parsons, a Virginia City gambler; Jim Gilchrist; Tilton Cockerell; and J.C. Roberts. A seventh man, Sol Jones, held the horses in the quarry as he waited for the arrival of the train with its masked passengers.

Marshall, the engineer, and the fireman were locked in the express car. "Be glad we didn't have to kill you," Davis said.

Earlier that day, Davis had received a coded telegram from John Chapman, the eighth gang member. Chapman had gone to San Francisco to find a train worth robbing. Then he sent back the telegram that Central Pacific No. 1 was the target.

The train had left Oakland behind its little red, wood-burning engine. After crossing the flatlands to Sacramento, an eight-wheeler helper locomotive assisted the train up the steep climb into the Sierras. With the train's slow travel, the robbers had plenty of time to position their getaway horses at the quarry and walk back to Verdi, where they knew the train would slow for the lumber siding. In fact a wrecked freight further up the line halted the express for two hours at Cisco, giving the robbers more time than they wanted on the clear, cold, November night. The delay of the train made possible the incredible coincidence of the West's first two train robberies—same train, same day, same state—and neither robbery connected to the other.

Back in Verdi, after his captors joined the others at the express-baggage car, conductor Mitchell realized that though he lacked an engine, he had downhill tracks to Reno, so he had the brakeman release the brakes. The engineer and fireman had broken out of the express car and were preparing to back up and recover the missing cars when they saw the cars approaching. The reunited train went on to Reno, called the police, and telegraphed the world that robbery had been added to western railroading.

With a new crew aboard, the train chugged on northeast. At 11:15 P.M., it pulled out of Independence, the third siding east of Wells, in the Pequop Mountains of Nevada. By now the full moon was covered with clouds; the shadows, not as sharp as earlier.

Suddenly, six men ran out from an old shed to jump aboard. They carried rifles in addition to revolvers. Although they knew nothing about the earlier robbery, they also detached the passenger cars. Six miles ahead—the tracks going uphill—the severed cars were far behind. The robbers threw off the fireman and messenger and ordered the engineer to keep going.

The robbers halted the engine and its one car near the Pequop siding and found the cargo pretty well picked over. They did get a silver bar, $1,400 in coin, and some mail. They jumped on their waiting horses and disappeared.

Conductor Carter on the second crew had heard passengers boast about what they would have done if they had been aboard the earlier train. When his cars were detached, he told the passengers they now had their chance. Passenger pistols mysteriously disappeared or suddenly became dysfunctional.

A small volunteer posse charged out into the night, searching for the robbers. What they found was the business half of the train, backing down to again connect with its rear half. As the train continued on east, pursuers on both Nevada's western and eastern borders now searched for two sets of robbers.

After the first robbery, the men divided the loot and disappeared into the moonlight shadows along the Truckee River. Davis headed south to Six Mile Canyon near Virginia City, some rode north, and three rode west, back through Verdi and up Sardine Valley toward California. Some carried coins in old boots used as temporary bags.

James H. Kinkead, Washoe County's undersheriff, was told that the first outlaws had headed south, but an all-day search of the Truckee-Carson City trail failed to produce a clue. Undaunted, Kinkead went back to Lawton's Springs, where the loot had been divided. He found a print from a narrow, high-heeled boot—a dandy's or gambler's boot—and followed that trail to Verdi. Kinkead had too many horse tracks to sort out, but he thought the outlaws must have walked back from Lawton's Springs, where they had left their horses, to where they would board the train. The wearer of the boots was one of them. Kinkead found no helpful clues at Verdi, but he had a hunch the robbers had headed into California. He continued northwest toward Nicholas Pearson's tavern in Sardine Valley.

Three of the robbers had stopped at the Pearson tavern late in the afternoon after the robbery. John Squires arrived first and alone. Shortly after, gambler Parsons and Jim Gilchrist, a miner having his first try at robbery, showed up together. They acted as though they did not know Squires. All three asked for supper and lodging.

Mrs. Pearson, a shrewd and curious woman, had seen a lot of men stay at the popular tavern. Something didn't seem right about these three. After twenty years of tavern keeping, she could judge people. Mrs. Pearson had heard about the robbery, and she watched closely. As she rocked her chair, she heard Squires walk across the hall to the room she had assigned to Parsons and Gilchrist. Strangers indeed! Now she would keep a sharper watch.

After breakfast, Squires and Parsons, still pretending to be strangers, checked out at the same time and rode northwest toward the Henness Pass trail into California. Then a deputy sheriff and a Wells Fargo agent arrived at Pearson's with questions. They asked if any guests had spent the night and moved on. Mrs. Pearson mentioned the two men riding toward California. The deputy and the agent followed.

Mrs. Pearson, still suspicious, continued to watch Gilchrist. As soon as the deputy and agent were out of sight, Gilchrist walked down to the outhouse behind the tavern. Mrs. Pearson slipped around to the women's side, where she knew the partition had a loose knot. This was no time for false modesty. She peeked through the knothole, and saw Gilchrist lower an old boot filled with twenty-dollar gold pieces into a convenient hiding place.

Shortly after Gilchrist returned to the tavern, he saw Mr. Pearson stroll down to the outhouse. A little later, Gilchrist looked again for his cache. It was gone.

Pearson ran for a sheriff, who was not hard to find in the area that morning. In fact, Undersheriff Kinkead had already found the unusual heel mark, followed it to Verdi, and was riding into Sardine Valley. He was near Pearson's tavern when Pearson came looking.

Kinkead found Gilchrist in the loft of Pearson's barn, but his boots didn't match the unusual heel mark. Kinkead did, however, persuade Gilchrist to talk freely about his associates. When Kinkead learned that one guest was the gambler Parsons, he was ready to bet that Parsons would be wearing the fancy boots.

Kinkead sent a deputy back to Reno with Gilchrist. Then, on the information from Gilchrist, he followed tracks through the snow to Loyalton, California, about 15 miles away. Slipping quietly into a tavern room recently rented to a stranger, Kinkead saw the man asleep in his bed. Very carefully, he extracted a pistol from under the man's pillow. Then he woke the stranger. It was the gambler Parsons, and his boots matched the heel mark.

With Parsons secured in a dependable saloon, Kinkead pushed on through a winter gale and darkness to Sierraville, 12 miles farther. There he found John Squires at his brother's farm. Without a thought about a Nevada officer making arrests in California, Kinkead handcuffed his suspects and took them to Reno.

Davis was arrested in Virginia City, and Roberts at a stage stop he operated at Antelope, just across the California line. Again, there were no complications with extradition. In those days the muzzle of a pistol was sufficient. Tilton Cockerill, a former army officer, and Sol Jones were arrested in a brothel in Reno.

Detectives in San Francisco and Oakland searched for the mysterious Chapman who had sent the coded message. Unable to find him, they took the next Central Pacific train to Reno. Unknown to them, Chapman was on the same train. When the detectives reached Reno, they stopped at a nearby tavern. So did Chapman, not knowing he was wanted. Then two local lawmen walked in with Sol Jones in their custody.

Seeing Chapman, Jones called out gaily, "Why hello, John. What brings you here?"

The detectives' prompt arrest of Chapman ended the two-state manhunt.

Gradually all but $3,000 of the $41,600 loss was recovered. The missing coins, if found today, would be worth over a half million dollars.

James B. Hume, Wells Fargo's chief detective, said the first robbery was "extremely well planned." The lookout in San Francisco with his coded telegraph message; the placing of the horses at the planned point of attack; the boarding of the train when it would have to slow down for the lumber siding; the separation of the cars to get the passengers, the conductor, and the brakeman out of the way; and the separation of the robbers into at least three getaway groups all support Hume's opinion.

Half of the eastern robbers presented no challenge. Three were deserters from nearby Camp Halleck. Posses with special engines and a company of cavalry from Camp Halleck followed a trail of newly minted half-dollars until the robbers were sighted in Utah. Mormon authorities captured two in the mountains near Salt Lake City and another in more open country, headed for Idaho. The other three, including two of the deserters, escaped.

Central Pacific No. 1 kept on chugging. For one day in Nevada, it had been a train of destiny.

Andrew Jackson
"Big Jack" Davis
Master Stage Robber

ndrew Jackson "Big Jack" Davis started out as an honest miner in the California Sierras. The intelligent, well-educated, fine-looking man, tall and strong, earned an excellent reputation that extended from the Tuolumne diggings as far north as Nevada and Sierra Counties. But he didn't find much gold, so he came to the Comstock Lode of Nevada Territory in late 1859, shortly after the discovery of silver there.

Perhaps Jack had grown tired of digging ore out of the ground in California. Blister-raising, knuckle-busting toil under the glaring sun of summer, followed by vainly seeking warmth in the thin tents pitched against the freezing winds of winter made many give up and return to eastern homes. They had seen the elephant and would let others seek riches in a forbidding land. Jack was willing to keep trying, but he had figured out that very few of those who made money in a mining camp were the ones who mined the ore. He wondered if he should try something different. When he reached Nevada, he built the first stable in Gold Hill.

Boarding horses for other people and renting out his own was easier than mining, but Jack soon tired of that, too—he tired of hunting for hay and grain, shoveling manure, repairing damaged buggies and wagons, and worrying about abuse to his own and leased horses. He moved over to Six Mile Canyon, a few miles east of Virginia City, leased a quartz mill, and built a cabin nearby.

A.J. "Big Jack" Davis
Nevada Historical Society, Reno

Now, he would grind the ore that others brought in, mix the pulverized product with mercury to extract the silver, and refine that amalgam into silver bullion. The work was still hard, but most of it could be done with heavy machinery operated by employees.

It appeared to outsiders that Jack prospered. He worked hard in his mill during the day, played poker in the evening, and became noted for his generous nature. Wanderers and wayfarers found his cabin door always open and his larder well-stocked. He was even elected recorder of claims for the Flowery Mining District. He might have been mistaken for a scholarly professor or a wealthy merchant. Judges, lawyers, and bankers welcomed him to their high-stakes poker games.

"That big fella sure looks out fer a man down on his luck," one hard-luck prospector would say.

"And he hob nobs with all them high muck-a-mucks, too. Jist like he was one of 'em."

But gradually, close observers of Davis's mill began wondering if he was shipping more bullion than could be reasonably extracted from the ore he seemed to be buying. He appeared to be a prosperous mill operator, but no one knew where he got his paying rock. He kept turning out a steady stream of bullion, and rumors even cropped up that the purpose of the mill was remelting and marketing bullion that had been obtained in robberies.

At that time, western mining communities disliked Wells Fargo for fares that seemed extortions to the people. They laughed at stage robberies, considering them a wrangle among thieves over spoils extracted from the common worker. When stages began hauling bullion out of the growing mining camps and returning currency to the mine owners and to the merchants so they could cash checks, the robberies increased. With stages coming into Virginia City from six or seven different directions, news of a robbery could be expected almost every day.

When a few people began wondering about Jack's source of prosperity, most just winked and nodded and said nothing that might reach the authorities. The Robin Hood possibility that their generous friend was taking advantage of the rich stage company was even more enjoyable when the masked robbers recruited by Jack added flair to their robberies.

On October 30, 1866, two stages traveling together moved out of Reno toward Virginia City. It was close to midnight, and the Sierra Range in the west was bathed in moonlight. The stages, each carrying seven passengers, rumbled past Steamboat Springs and out onto the Washoe Plain.

The lead coach, driven by John Burnett, carried a large express chest made of boilerplate bolted securely to the frame of the coach. Its six horses labored up the winding Geiger Grade with the other coach close behind. They topped the grade at a slow walk 3 miles north of Virginia City. Before the horses could catch their breath and trot on into town, five masked men stepped forward out of the rocks and sagebrush.

"Hold up," one shouted, waving his shotgun. Some carried Henry rifles.

Burnett's foot hit the brake, and the relieved horses stopped and breathed deeply, their ribs heaving as they sucked in the cool mountain air.

"Better point that gun the other way, young feller," Burnett said. "It might go off, you know."

"Well we don't want to shoot you but will if you don't follow orders."

"Your passengers, too," another said, nodding his head.

The leader stepped up and spoke in a gruff voice, obviously trying to disguise it. "You will all step down, as we have some business to transact with Wells Fargo. You drivers unhitch and move your horses a ways up the canyon. This will take us some time and some blasting powder."

The fourteen passengers filed down from the coaches. Only one was armed, and he tried to keep his revolver hidden. Another tossed his wallet and its $400 to the roof of his coach. No one noticed. But the robbers got the $60 from his pocket and another $60 from Judge Baldwin. They made similar extractions from the other passengers, but not from either driver or from the only woman passenger, "You fellows work hard for your pay," the leader said to the drivers, "and don't get much anyhow. And this young lady here"—he bowed deeply—"is also excused from the evening's business. The rest of you just stand aside and don't get in our way."

The woman, a Miss Crowell, was returning from a shopping trip to San Francisco, and she clutched her hoop skirt carefully as she tried to find a level place to stand. The leader of the robbers gently took her elbow and led her to a rock while another robber brought a cushion out from the coach.

"Now, you just sit here young lady," the leader said. "We won't bother you at all." He looked at one of his men. "Bring out a lap robe for the lady. The air is cool and we have work to do." He bowed and made sure she was comfortable while two men climbed into the forward coach with hammers and cold chisels.

Two of the masked robbers chiseled the hasp off the iron express box. While they worked, others brought out overcoats and more robes. Then someone found a small cargo of champagne in a rear boot.

The leader looked at his watch. "Now would you look at that—just what we need. It's Halloween, exactly two years to the day since President Lincoln signed Nevada into the good old U. S. of A. This calls for libations while we work, and let's pour some for the little lady, too. We'll start with a toast to Miss Crowell."

As the two men continued working on the hasp and another kept the drivers and passengers under close watch, the leader and another handed out champagne. They drank toasts to Miss Crowell, to President Lincoln, to Wells Fargo, to the Comstock Lode, and to the new state of Nevada. Then, two cans of blasting powder were packed around the express box's lock and a long fuse installed and ignited. Miss Crowell covered her ears and grimaced until the loud blast shook the air. The coach trembled as though held by a large giant. The blast blew out the end of the box and ignited the inside of the coach, but the robbers threw dirt in until the fire went out. Then they scooped out $5,000 from the box and added it to the coin and watches they already had.

"You'll have to finish the party without the pleasure of our company," the leader said, as they ran to where their horses were securely tied.

The passengers all got back into the undamaged coach. The lead coach wobbled like a drunk out too late at night as the coaches and passengers moved on to Virginia City. They arrived about 3 A.M. with another tale of Nevada stage robbing.

But some passengers had heard enough of Big Jack Davis's talk, even though he tried to disguise his voice, that they reported their impressions to the police. No one listened more sympathetically to the stories about the holdup next day than Big Jack. Finally he was arrested, but the jury refused to convict.

But Wells Fargo began putting shotgun-carrying messengers on their stages, and the bandits had more to think about than one busy driver with four or six horses under his control. After they began adding an occasional second messenger, Big Jack started looking for a supplementary source of income. Robbing stages had become a hazardous occupation!

He studied the operations of trains coming east out of Oakland through Reno to carry silver and gold to eastern destinations. He gathered seven confederates, and he planned and carried out the West's first train robbery. Although the overall planning and the coordination between confederates were superb, a curious woman innkeeper and a skilled lawman combined to put the entire gang into custody in less than four days after the 1870 robbery. Davis confessed and showed the officers where he had hidden almost $20,000 in a culvert, a short distance from the robbery site.

Officers on the Comstock had suspected that Big Jack and John Squires, one of the train robbers, had been involved in many holdups of Wells Fargo stages in the area for years. But every time their work was sufficient to bring the robbers before a jury, the jury would be convinced that a reasonable doubt existed and would acquit. The railroad robbery turned out differently. Two men were released after they testified against the others. Squiers got the longest sentence, twenty-three years. Four others got sentences of twenty-two, twenty, eighteen, and five years. Big Jack Davis, the leader, got ten, entering the prison on Christmas Day.

Davis claimed with righteous indignation that Wells Fargo had forced him into train robbery when it put so many shotgun messengers as guards on its stages.

Davis was pardoned early. In 1871, less than nine months after his sentence began, twenty-nine inmates of the Nevada State Prison, broke out in the largest prison escape in the West. They included four of Davis's train-robbing accomplices. They did not include Davis or the man who got the five-year sentence.

Davis could have gone out of the prison, but he refused. He cooperated with prison officials, and was pardoned on February 16, 1875, after P.C. Hyman, the prison warden, wrote to the board of pardons and explained Davis's help in investigating the escape. His letter said that Davis's conduct had been exemplary and it ended: "If good conduct is to be taken into consideration, in my judgment he deserves the leniency of the board." One week later, Davis was released.

But Big Jack Davis hadn't forgotten his difficulty in earning an honest living. He returned to stage robbery, again determined to use his fine mind in outwitting Wells Fargo. He had never worried about the stage driver, whose first concern was controlling his horses. He worried about the messengers whose only concern was fighting off robbers, and he particularly wanted to know whether the stage carried one or two messengers. One messenger usually rode on the seat behind the driver, and a second messenger would ride inside the coach. So, if Big Jack knew that the stage had one messenger and the driver was alone on the seat, or that it had two messengers, he would look out for the armed man or men inside the coach.

Big Jack decided that a signaling system would enable a confederate, seeing the stage leave a station, to signal how many messengers were aboard to the robbers who lay in wait on the stage road. And he realized that such a system would work better in the sparsely settled country of eastern Nevada. There, the confederate, after a stage left at night, could hurry to a nearby mountain and signal with small fires about the number of messengers. One fire meant one messenger aboard, and two meant a pair.

Big Jack's well organized plan worked fine until September 3, 1877. On that day, Jack's signaler, Tom Lauria, watched the stage leave Eureka in the evening dusk, southbound for Tybo. Lauria saw two messengers get aboard, and he hurried to his horse and galloped away toward Pancake Mountain.

Big Jack with two brothers named Hamilton rode up to the Willows Station, 40 miles south of Eureka. This first station on the road to the Tybo mines was usually tended by William Hood, a horse wrangler and blacksmith. The three masked bandits crept up on Hood and a surprised visiting rancher, Josh Tingley, who had stopped at the station to visit. Jack and the Hamilton brothers bound and gagged their two prisoners and tied them to a center post in the barn. Then they waited, watching for the signal that Tom Lauria would light on Pancake Peak, 10 miles away.

Well after dusk had turned to darkness, Eugene Blair, riding as messenger behind the driver on the stage to Tybo, looked up and spoke.

"Jack, you see that star low in the sky over there?" He pointed. "I never did see one right there before."

Driver Jack Perry looked and responded. "Probably a hunter out late on Pancake Peak. Got him a fire to keep warm."

"Maybe so."

"It'll be a cool one tonight." Perry shivered.

At about nine o'clock, the stage approached Willows Station and Big Jack recognized Blair, riding as messenger behind the driver. Big Jack stepped out of the darkness at the barn and shouted, "Blair. Throw up your hands."

Eugene Blair was a good man and a determined one. Seven months before, while working on the Hamilton to Ward stage run about 40 miles east of his present route, his stage had been held up by two men as it approached the Ward station. He wounded one robber, but the other fled. He carried the wounded man into Ward, where he died. Then, Blair returned to the holdup site to follow the tracks of the other bandit. Ten days later, lighter in weight, his skin darkened by the winter sun and his chapped lips grimly set, he returned to Ward Station, his prisoner in tow.

This time, as Blair's stage approached the Willows Station, he was on his usual alert. When he heard the surrender demand, he jumped down, shifted his shotgun to his right hand, and crouched instinctively. The blast from Davis's two shotgun barrels seemed to slam into Blair's body, but the lead sailed overhead. Then he felt Davis's shotgun muzzle push against his chest.

Eugene Blair had never lost a fight and didn't intend to lose this one. He knew he was fighting Big Jack Davis, the brainiest bandit in Nevada. Blair grabbed the gun barrels and swung Davis around. He grappled with Davis, looking for an opening. He could see another man dancing about in the darkness, trying for a clear shot at him. Then he spun Davis squarely into the light from the stage's lamps, jumped away, and shouted, "Get him Jimmy."

Jimmy Brown, the second and unexpected messenger, shot from inside the stage, and Big Jack Davis fell in the dust and darkness. As Brown put his foot on a wheel to jump down, one of the Hamiltons shot him in the leg. The other Hamilton never appeared. Presumably he held the bandits' horses.

Tom Lauria's two fires were either too close together or at the wrong angle for viewing from Willows Station. They had appeared as one fire from 10 miles away.

Blair and the stage driver released the wrangler and his visitor, tied up in the barn. Then they carried Davis and Brown into the station cabin.

"We got to be going on," the driver said to Blair. "Will yuh have to stay here with Jimmy and the prisoner? Yuh know what we got in the cargo."

"You don't seem to be hurt bad, Jimmy," Blair said, turning to Brown. Reckon you can keep an eye on Big Jack until the morning stage gets in from Tybo? You could haul him back to Eureka on it."

"I'll be fine," Brown said. I been hurt worse in the mines. I'll see he gets back to the sheriff in Eureka."

"You take care now, Jimmy," Blair called out as he climbed back on the stage. He spoke to the driver as he pulled up his collar against the evening chill. "Don't look like Big Jack's gonna rob any more stages for a while."

"He didn't rob this'n, thanks to you and Jimmy." The driver slapped the reins down on the horses' rumps, and the stage moved away.

Davis had nine buckshot in his back, and he begged, in his intense agony, to be mercifully killed. Brown's wound was painful but not dangerous. The northbound stage had one passenger when it made its brief stop the next forenoon. He helped load the two wounded men in for the trip back to Eureka.

As the stage lumbered along, crossing the high, rocky, sagebrush-covered land, the September sun glistened from distant hills. Andrew Jackson Davis wondered how he could have misread the signal. Tom Lauria was a good man. He must have seen the two messengers on the stage.

Davis thought the air should warm as the sun rose into the sky, but he shivered as he shifted his weight to get comfortable. A back full of buckshot did pain a man. The wounded messenger would get well, but what about him? He had never been hurt so bad.

Brown looked out the window, ignoring his enemy, but the stage's lone paying passenger stared at Big Jack with contempt.

"To hell with him and the rest of the world," Big Jack might have thought. "I tried to be better than the rest, but sometimes they just had better luck. That Eugene Blair was some kind of a man in a fight."

When the stage reached Page's Ranch early in the afternoon, it turned into a hearse. Big Jack Davis, the smartest stage robber in Nevada, had reached the end of his career.

Prison Riot

In 1871 the Nevada State Prison occupied part of the building housing the Warm Springs Hotel in the southeast part of Carson City. Its iron cells opened out to a large room where the inmates ate and lounged when they were not confined to their cells or had work duties. At 6 P.M. on Sunday, September 17, Volney E. Rollins, captain of the guard, entered the large room alone to lock the inmates in their cells for the night. Several of them, their escape plans complete, lay in wait.

Frank Clifford, serving ten years for horse stealing, led the other twenty-eight rioters. They had armed themselves with metal billy clubs, made by enclosing chunks of iron in pieces of cloth ripped from their clothing and fastened to their wrists with cloth loops, or lanyards. Others carried homemade knives.

When Rollins stepped through the door, one inmate crashed a bottle down on his head from behind, leaving a long gash, while another smashed him over the left eye with his homemade billy, cutting to the bone. Rollins slumped to the floor, barely conscious, and other inmates quickly closed the door, so no alarm resulted.

Vicious men with nothing to lose moved in for the kill, but inmate Pat Hurley bravely grabbed the captain, dragged him to a cell, threw him in, and locked the door, undoubtedly saving the officer's life. The rioters did get the captain's keys before Hurley dragged him to safety.

Then, the escapers climbed to the top of the upper tier of cells and broke a hole through the ceiling. They pulled each other through and rushed along the attic to a position above the office of Deputy Warden Zimmerman. He was asleep, and the noise of the inmates breaking through his ceiling woke him up. Zimmerman fled in fear and was criticized later for cowardice.

Clifford and his men then ran to the armory, unlocked it with

Nevada State Prison
Nevada Historical Society, Reno

Captain Rollins's keys, and armed themselves with two Henry rifles, four double-barreled shotguns, and five revolvers, plus 3,000 rounds of ammunition for the Henry rifles.

Then the rioters plunged down a stairway, leading to a room that adjoined the apartment of Lieutenant Governor Frank Denver and his family. By virtue of his office, Denver served as the prison's warden. Mr. and Mrs. Denver, plus several lady and one or two gentleman guests were just sitting down to dinner. The noise frightened the ladies, who thought the uproar was caused by an earthquake. They jumped up from their chairs.

Bob Dedman, an inmate trusty with a life sentence, served as Denver's waiter. He and Denver immediately ran to the next room and saw the rioters starting to crowd down the stairs. Denver shot Clifford in the abdomen with his derringer, and then ran to another room to get his revolver.

In the meantime Bob Dedman grabbed a wood-bottomed chair and crashed it down to make it into a weapon. He was swinging it manfully against the men on the stairs when Denver returned with his revolver.

Denver opened fire and kept blasting away until he went down with a shot to the leg and blows to his head from rifles and sharp weapons. One of his wounds penetrated his skull; another left a 4-inch gash in his forehead.

Dedman had his chair weapon jerked out of his hands. As he paused to get another, he saw the ladies peering through the door. He stopped long enough to shoo them towards safety and then returned to the battle with a second chair. He knocked down at least five inmates, one of them going over the balustrade above as the battle seesawed up and down the stairs. His heroic conduct clearly saved the life of the lieutenant governor. Dedman was finally knocked unconscious, and the rioters poured past him toward the yard.

Since it was Sunday with no work requirements and no inmates in the yard, the reduced guard staff did not include any men along the outer wall. The noise from the rioters fighting Dedman and Denver provided the first notice of the outbreak.

P.M. Isaacs, a guard from Gold Hill, faced the rioters and fired his revolver as they debouched into the yard. He stood like a stone statue, pouring his bullets into the crowd of men. When he got shot in his right knee, breaking his leg, he shifted his weight to the left and kept on shooting. But a shot to his hip brought him down. The inmates grabbed his revolver but spared his life out of admiration for his courage.

Meanwhile, John Newhouse, also a guard from Gold Hill, charged to the sound of the guns and opened fire with his revolver. His first shot dropped E.B. Parsons, one of the Verdi train robbers of less than a year before. But Newhouse fell himself an instant later with one wound in the back of his head and another in his back.

By this time, a Virginia City guard named Perasich had joined the battle. Outside the yard and unarmed when he heard the first shots, Perasich hurried into the hotel, got a five-shot revolver, and ran back into the yard, firing away. His first three shots sent three men staggering, but as he fired the fourth, an inmate's bullet entered his left hip, traveled down the thigh, and lodged between the artery and the bone. He fell to the ground, out of the fight and helpless, at the prison door.

Also in the fight by this time was Matt Pixley, one of the hotel proprietors. Hearing the shooting, he grabbed a revolver and ran into the yard with Perasich to assist the officers. Most of the rioters were still inside the guard room, shooting at Isaacs, Newhouse, and Perasich through the main door. Pixley ran to a window and began shooting into the room, when Charles Jones fired back with one of the stolen Henry rifles. The shot passed through two panes of glass, hit Pixley below the left eye, passed all the way through his head, and dropped him dead.

Then R.W. Bergerser, one of Pixley's bartenders, joined the battle and had three close escapes. Two shots whizzed by his ears and a third struck the crotch of his pants, taking out both the seats of his pants and his underdrawers.

Another guard, a little Frenchman named Henri, fought and escaped without a scratch. He fired all the ammunition he had into the crowd and then rushed in to swing his weapon as a club until all the rioters were outside the wall. His clothing was cut to shreds by return fire, but he was never hit.

At about 7:00 P.M., when the full extent of the break was known and twenty-nine inmates had scattered into the countryside, the organized militia at Virginia City was called out. They arrived by special train three hours later. In the meantime, a large force of citizens met at the state armory in Carson City, drew arms and ammunition, and began their patrols. Some went to the prison to prevent a return attack; others patrolled the city's streets. Perhaps the citizens at the prison feared the escapers would return for more weapons and ammunition.

At 9:20 P.M., a rider left to warn Genoa's residents. When he saw two inmates appearing to aim a gun at him, he wheeled and rode out of range.

Twenty-seven National Guardsmen and fifteen organized militiamen arrived at 10:00 P.M. By shortly after midnight, mounted patrols were riding out from Carson City in every direction.

Late Monday afternoon, eighteen of the escaped prisoners were seen on a hill about 10 miles southeast of the prison, and a blacksmith southeast of town on the Carson River reported that six men had forced him to remove their irons. One of them had a leg wound. Thomas Carter, an Elko train robber, was captured that Monday, the day after the escape.

John Squires, a Verdi train robber, and one other man were found in a small cave northeast of Virginia City on September 27, ten days after the escape. The Virginia City police chief and other officers had been scouting the area for several days, and they had noticed signs of men raiding vegetable gardens. The two men gave up quickly. Squiers told the officers that if they were allowed to go, they would leave the country and never return and would send the officers every cent they made for the next three years. The officers laughed and took them in.

Four more were captured together the next day. They included Frank Clifford, the leader, and two more Verdi train robbers, E.B. Parsons and J.E. Chapman. The four men were brought in to Dayton by rancher W.H. Burgess and his hired man, Edward J. Healy, in a small two-horse wagon. They had been captured on Burgess's ranch, 75 miles east of Virginia City with the help of a small group of Paiute Indians. The prisoners told Burgess that all they had to eat since their escape was one scrawny coyote, and they were tired of being stalked by curious Indians.

David Lynch, another man captured on September 28, was placed in the Ormsby County jail to await his trial for the escape. But he escaped again from the jail and never was recaptured.

Two nights later, Chris Blair and Billy Forrest were seen on the Geiger Grade, north of Virginia City. Blair went into a brewery for a drink while Forrest stood guard outside. A man recognized them and ran for the sheriff, who took up the trail the next day. Shortly after the sheriff sighted them, the convicts plunged into a thick canyon where the sheriff's horses could not follow. More than two years would pass before Blair was found. Forrest was never found.

Three more men were captured in early October.

By then, word had reached Carson City of a gun battle on September 24 in Inyo County, California, 120 miles south. Shortly before the battle, Verdi train robbers Chat Roberts and Tilton Cockerill, along with four others, had killed a mounted mailman to get his horse. Then, California citizens fought them in a pitched battle at Mount Diablo Lake. They changed its name to Convict Lake, which it still bears. Californian Robert Morrison was killed in the battle and his name given to a nearby mountain.

Two of the men in the Inyo County battle, Elko train robber Leander Morton and Moses Black, were hanged by vigilantes at Bishop, California. Roberts, eighteen, feared vigilante execution but he was spared, apparently because of his youth. One of this group, Charles Jones who had killed Pixley, escaped the captors and was never found. The other survivors, including Cockerill and Roberts, were returned to prison.

Prison records for the time are not complete, but it appears that, besides Jones who escaped from his captors and Lynch who escaped again while waiting trial for the first escape, six more inmates were never found.

Prison records are available for some of the men who later asked for pardons and had to explain their offenses while in prison. Three of these claimed that they just walked out the door after it had been left open by the escapers. They weren't planning to leave; they just couldn't pass up the opportunity that had dropped in their laps. Considering the circuitous route followed by the escapers and the fierce opposition they faced, this claim probably got little attention from the Board of Pardons.

William Willis, one of the earliest recaptured, did get a pardon in 1879. His pardon recited that he had originally surrendered and pled guilty to arson to save being hanged by vigilantes. Perhaps his early capture resulted from his memory that prison had once looked like a safe haven for him. His certificate of pardon did not mention his escape.

The Nevada State Prison is still located in the same part of town, but it is no longer part of a hotel.

Nicanor Rodrigues
The Spanish King

Nicanor Rodrigues was born into the hidalgo class in the mountains of Spain about 1840. He inherited from his father, an important member of the aristocracy, the class's noble disdain for labor or business. After living for a time in both Paris and Rome, he told his father that he wanted to follow the examples of ancestors who had spread Spanish influence to the new world. His father gave the boy, barely a teenager, a few hundred pesos and wished him well in Mexico City.

But Nicanor found life dull in the capital of New Spain, and he followed the gold rush north to California. Seeking excitement without the drudgery of manual labor or the boredom of business, he joined a band of robbers operating in the northern mines. The leader of the band had been as unusual in his choice of a second profession as his newest neophyte—aged fifteen—was in the choice of his first.

Dr. Thomas J. Hodges had just graduated from medical school in Tennessee when he joined the army to serve in the war against Mexico. But instead of going home after the war to start a medical practice, he followed the gold rush to California, changed his name to Tom Bell, and recruited a band of robbers. The well-educated southerner may have felt a bond with the highborn Spanish youth. We don't know how long Nicanor was in Bell's band, but it was long enough for one robbery and a shootout.

On March 12, 1856, five of Bell's men, including Nicanor, robbed four travelers in the Trinity Alps of northwestern California. Exactly a month later a different band of Bell's robbers, not including Nicanor, held up a stage near Marysville, California. In the investigation that followed, robber William Carter was found with a watch that had been taken in the earlier robbery. This led to a shootout when police barged in to a tent-cabin near Folsom on April 24. The police fired twenty-five shots, killing one robber and wounding Nicanor twice. A third robber escaped.

Nicanor fired two shots before he fell with bullets in his arm and his leg. The police found four pistols, a double-barreled shotgun and a large bowie knife in the tent-cabin.

Sentenced to the California State Prison for ten years, Nicanor was moved to Angel Island in San Francisco Bay, then the location of the prison. When the authorities learned that he was barely sixteen, they notified the governor and he granted the boy a pardon. Young in years but old in ambition and determination, Nicanor went immediately to the Comstock in Nevada.

The bright young man thought that wealth should be collected at its source and had no interest in robbing individuals of small amounts. So, he turned his attention to the quartz mills that refined gold and silver bullion from the ore that hard-working peons dug from the ground. One of his earliest adventures in Nevada was the theft of precious amalgam from the retorts of the Imperial Mill at Gold Hill. Later, he removed an entire wheelbarrow load of amalgam from the Pacific Mill. He buried it in the Silver City cemetery until the uproar about the brazen theft died down.

Nicanor's most daring robbery occurred when he saw three bricks of silver bullion being loaded into the front boot on the Virginia City to Reno stage. He ran into the stage office, bought passage on the stage, and asked the driver, Baldy Green, if he could ride on the box with him. Baldy's stage had been robbed so often that miners had made up a ballad about "Baldy, Hand Down the Express Box," but this time no one would stop the stage and make such a demand. Of course, Baldy let him ride on the box. He had heard about the linguistic skills of the young Spaniard, and he looked forward to some highfalutin conversation.

The spur of the moment robbery demonstrated the skill of a dashing young man who saw in other people's carelessness opportunities for sudden wealth that others missed. Taking advantage of those opportunities with courage and skill was, to Nicanor, his right. He felt more entitled to the world's wealth than the unimaginative people who produced it.

When the stage left the long Geiger Grade and turned north on the flat meadows of Steamboat Springs, Nicanor diverted Baldy's attention by asking him if he could see an eagle flying in the distance or something on the mountains to the west. Then he quickly and silently extracted a brick from the boot and dropped it over the side into the roadside dust. He seared into his memory the appearance of the roadside willows and sagebrush that marked the location.

The audacious bandit repeated his actions twice more, each time after diverting Baldy's attention by some innocuous question. When the stage reached Reno, Nicanor hurried to the nearest stable and rented a team and buggy. He drove back up the stage road and made the three stops necessary to recover his treasure before Baldy knew it was gone or anyone else had seen the bricks lying along the road.

This time, however, suspicion implicated Baldy's passenger. When Nicanor left the bricks at an assay office in Gold Hill to be melted into smaller ingots, the assayer told him to come back in a few days. Nicanor, immediately suspicious that something was amiss, forgot about the bricks and quickly moved his operations out of town.

Nicanor did not know that the Washoe County sheriff had found his fresh buggy tracks and followed them the next morning to the assay office. There the officers learned that an unidentified man had left the bricks and was told to return. They posted a guard, but, of course, their suspect never showed up.

Although Nicanor never considered Mexicans socially equal to hidalgos like him with pure Spanish blood, Nevada's Mexicans treated him as a folk hero. He became a legendary Robin Hood who robbed the rich and gave to the poor. This adulation from Mexican workers seems strange. By the time the debonair young man left Virginia City, he was noted for hosting elaborate dinners, where he displayed the most impeccable taste in the town's best restaurants. He often asked them to serve wild game accompanied by the best European wine. A handsome man, Nicanor invited the area's loveliest ladies and its most esteemed young gentlemen to his soirees, entertaining them with his quick wit and worldly conversation. Suave and cultured, he captivated his guests with stories of European and other capitals. But he did not have the reputation of opening his door to down-on-the-luck miners that Andrew Jackson "Big Jack" Davis enjoyed.

Contemporaries on the Comstock, both Nicanor—by now called the Spanish King—and Big Jack led double lives. Each hobnobbed with law-abiding judges, bankers, and public officials until suspicion of criminal activities became too strong and forced them into the open. While Big Jack patronized the wealthy and powerful, he kept his door open to the poor, something the Spanish King did not do. So it is surprising that the Mexican workingmen thought of him as a Robin Hood.

The two men differed in another respect. Davis was finally sent to prison. Nicanor, while arrested many times, was never convicted.

Nicanor was known for his immaculate dress and his Old World manners. The budding young socialite women, in the beginning, had individual dreams of conquering the cultured young Spaniard. And he soon added to his laurels the beauty of his chosen mistress. We don't know her name, but she worshiped her dashing young lover. This, too, has a strange element. She was a Mormon woman and brought up in the strict moral demands of that faith.

Nicanor's prejudice against operating a business apparently abated after he discovered some of the handicaps of a criminal career. After leaving Virginia City in 1867, he stopped in Austin and set up a saloon in partnership with Jack Harris, another robber of Wells Fargo stages and an all-around bandit on the Comstock. In fact, it was Harris's cabin to which Billy Mayfield moved Henry Plummer, the California fugitive, to hide him from Marshal John Blackburn. Eventually, Plummer, a notorious Montana sheriff, was hanged by vigilantes on his own gallows.

But the Austin mining camp fell on hard times, and several rich strikes had just been made at Hamilton and Treasure Hill, farther east. The partners closed their saloon, and the Spanish King moved on with his mistress to White Pine County. In a few years Harris, too, would be hanged by vigilantes.

Shortly after Nicanor arrived in White Pine County, he robbed the Shermantown Mill of a sack of amalgam. A posse of 250 men scoured White Pine County for the robber and found Nicanor. But he hired his close friend and former fellow socialite back in Virginia City, Judge Jesse Pitzer, to come and defend him. The evidence seemed clear to the police, but Pitzer argued to the jury that a man of Nicanor's stature would never run around with hoodlums. The jury agreed and acquitted—one of a long line of acquittals that the Spanish King would eventually receive.

Nicanor returned to stage robbing. He concentrated on the Gilmer and Saulsbury stage line. Agents for Wells Fargo, this line covered eastern Nevada from Pioche all the way north to Battle Mountain. Two or three holdups a week were soon reported, not all, of course, by one band of robbers.

But more and more the drivers mentioned a handsome young man leading the robbers. By this time Wells Drury, ace reporter for the *Territorial Enterprise*, considered Nicanor the king of Nevada stage robbers. But with pressure increasing from more frequent arrests, in 1872 Nicanor moved his operations again, this time to Pioche, the busiest mining camp in Nevada. There, two of the half dozen or so inmates from the 1871 prison escape appeared to have joined his gang. We don't know who they were, but none of the men who escaped and remained uncaptured had Mexican names.

Booming Pioche had doubled its population in four months. Prices soared as beef became scarce. At first, Nicanor's men rustled steers in

Old Lincoln County Courthouse, Pioche, Nevada
Nevada Historical Society, Reno

Utah, drove them over the state line, and sold them to butchers in Pioche. But he soon returned to stage robbery.

Nicanor and his men stopped a stage 2 miles from Pioche one night and found the express box nearly empty. After robbing all the passengers, they took the mail sacks and got $2,000 that was being mailed to Nevada State Bank. This time Nicanor was arrested and charged.

But the jury acquitted him after a dozen of his friends supported his claim of an alibi. However, the same stage was robbed a week later, and this time Nicanor fled to the mountains. Officers and posses tracked him through the mountains for several weeks and were about to give up when Nicanor sent word to Gilmer and Saulsbury that he was tired of being hunted and would like to negotiate an agreement with them.

By this time Gilmer and Saulsbury had been reduced to the brink of bankruptcy. They were willing to do most anything to stop the robberies. They sent word to Nicanor that they were ready to deal. Nicanor sent a Mexican guide to bring their representative to him.

The stage company sent its lawyer, Colonel W.W. Bishop to meet the Mexican. Bishop described the meeting:

"A young Mexican acted as my guide. We left Pioche on burros at midnight and went over Spring Mountain. Taking a long sweep to the right we soon struck a rugged ravine and started up it. I could see armed Mexicans behind every clump of sagebrush. We passed safely through the defile until we reached a grove of stunted pines. These, we found, hid the entrance to a natural cave or tunnel, which ran into the side of the mountain.

"Our burros were tied behind the trees, and torches were furnished to us by an old woman who emerged from the darkness of the cavern. After going about seventy-five yards into the tunnel my guide whistled, and seven or eight big fellows came cautiously out from behind the rocks and advanced to meet us. Without a word they seized a large flat stone, which looked like a part of the floor of the tunnel and, moving it aside, disclosed a lower chamber, oval in shape and about the size of an ordinary church.

"A ladder was thrust up, and following my guide downward I found myself in the presence of Nicanor and some dozen or so of his most trusted friends, several women being of the number.

"Nick was very brief. He said all he wanted was to be left alone. If the stage line and the express company would let up on him and not prosecute him, he would protect their property until one side or the other should see fit to terminate the contract, in which case fair notice should be given. I was authorized to act, and at once agreed to his terms."

It was rumored that the stage company had agreed to pay Nicanor $2,000 a month besides, but they never admitted that. A few days later, Nicanor appeared in Pioche and told Colonel B.F. Sides, the stage agent, "If I can prevent it, your stages will never be stopped as long as you're the agent here."

Nicanor kept his word, and the stage line's holdups decreased. But when the company sent a new agent to Pioche, Nicanor terminated the agreement, giving the company fair notice of his decision. He called on the new agent, one Seibert.

"I am very regretful, Señor, but I am no longer able to take care of your treasure boxes. You must protect your own property."

Then the robberies resumed.

But Nicanor was finally arrested and bail was so high he could not post it. Feeling that conviction and imprisonment was near, he escaped with the help of two other prisoners. They knocked the jailer down as he made his nightly round of inspections. The jailer fired his pistol, and they knocked him unconscious. They stole some horses in Spring Valley, and rode to the Utah ranch of Mormon James Maxwell on the headwaters of the Sevier River.

After a period of rest, and perhaps to return for his mistress, Nicanor and one of his co-escapers, Eugene Billieu, a Frenchman, returned to within a dozen miles of Pioche, robbed a stage, stole more horses from the C.H. Light ranch, and quietly returned to Utah. There, they picked up the other escaper, a horse thief named Yank, and headed for Mexico.

Like all of us, Nicanor learned to compromise as he grew older. He gave up his ideal of stealing wealth only from its source. First, he shifted away from the quartz mills, which he thought exploited their workers, and began robbing the express boxes on the stagecoaches. From this to robbing the passengers may have seemed to him a small step at the time.

But the compromise he made as he fled to Mexico was unusual indeed. All Nicanor's followers thought their leader, with his charmed life, could be trusted for his loyalty. Billieu, who only robbed with

Nicanor once, and Yank, merely a horse thief, were fleeing from the law together, and they reasonably expected loyalty from their co-escaper. When Nicanor's last pursuers from Nevada got 50 miles south of Maxwell's ranch, they found Billieu and Yank dead. They had been shot in the back by the man they trusted, obviously to make it harder for lawmen to follow.

A miner who had once worked in Pioche returned from Sinaloa in 1888 and reported that a man he thought was Nicanor had a huge ranch in the mountains near Mazatlán. He had a large band of horses and called himself Don Felipe Castro Estrada. But the miner wasn't sure, and he said nothing about the man having a mistress.

If the man was Nicanor Rodrigues, his years of robbing mills, stages, and people in Nevada probably contributed to a small fortune that the once proud hidalgo, who turned into a back-stabbing killer, was finally able to invest in Mexico upon his retirement.

———Milton Sharp———
Hunting Gold in Dalzell Canyon

Milton Sharp considered stage robbery a craft to be mastered. No one did it better than he. Drury Wells, editor of the Virginia City *Territorial Enterprise*, interviewed Sharp after one of his arrests and called him the most industrious highwayman in all of Nevada. "He robbed stages whenever he wanted to," Wells wrote, "and with great thoroughness, never making a mistake and never finding an empty treasure box."

Missouri born, part Cherokee and part French, Sharp was a veteran of the Confederate Army with five bullet- and bayonet-scars. He stood 5 feet, 5 inches tall, had brown eyes, brown hair, and a neat mustache and goatee. His dark good looks, cultured speech, and charming manners impressed all. A man of good habits, he never gambled, he shunned tobacco, and only took a drink when a friend offered and then only if he didn't have to accept a second one. His one bad habit was robbing stages, particularly in Nevada's Dalzell Canyon north of the Aurora, Nevada, and Bodie, California, mines. He usually worked alone.

Sharp had been a miner for twelve years when, at thirty-four, he turned to robbing stages for a living. Before that, he had tried to improve himself by studying bookkeeping in night school. His criminal career coincided with years of heavy production from the Aurora, Bodie, and Candelaria mines. Wells Fargo stages hauled practically all that production 90 miles north to the United States mint in Carson.

Wells Fargo did not expect its drivers to resist robbers. They had their hands full driving four-horse and six-horse teams. Shotgun-carrying messengers, some on top of the coach, some inside, protected stages car-

Milton Sharp
Wells Fargo Bank, N.A.

rying bullion. Somehow Sharp knew which stages those were, and he left them alone. He preferred stages going *to* the mines with less treasure and less protection. Occasionally, he encountered a stage with a messenger, either protecting a mine payroll or returning to the mines for another assignment. But he only shot one messenger, and that man would ride with him when Sharp finally was delivered to prison. Apparently, he considered shooting, except in self-defense, below his dignity.

Sharp preferred working alone, but broke that rule in Dalzell Canyon on June 8, 1880, when he and a helper, Frank Dow, met the southbound stage as it climbed up the canyon approaching Aurora and Bodie. Sharp stepped out from the cottonwoods and willows along the East Walker River and stopped the stage. In a well-modulated, polite voice, he told the passengers—they included one messenger—to step out and line up in a straight line.

"Keep your backs to me and the stage," he said. With Dow watching the driver, Sharp continued, "Just drop your cash, watches, and jewelry on the ground and take three steps forward. Keep your eyes straight ahead. The first one to turn around will be shot so dead, he'll be ready for skinning."

After selecting several watches and about $100 from the passengers, he took the gold watch of driver Tom Chamberlain and the express box containing $3,000 in coin. Then he excused himself, and he and Dow disappeared into the sagebrush. The passengers agreed that Sharp had been very business-like. He was always gallant to lady passengers, who said he acted like a high-toned gentlemen.

A posse of law officers, Wells Fargo detectives and messengers, and Paiute Indians tracked Sharp and Dow all the way to Walker Lake, before the trail grew cold.

Exactly a week after that robbery, and back in Dalzell Canyon again, Sharp and Dow robbed another stage driven by Chamberlain and bound for Aurora and Bodie. This time they took only the express box, leaving the passengers alone. They told Chamberlain where he could find the box, without its contents, on his return trip.

"We don't want to put you to any inconvenience, having to search for it," Sharp told Chamberlain. "And as soon as we find it convenient, we'll return your fine watch and also the watches that we took from your passengers last week. We don't really need them."

History does not tell us if the watches were returned.

An hour later Chamberlain met the northbound stage. It carried a consignment of bullion, protected by three shotgun-carrying messengers. Hearing Chamberlain's report, they checked their weapons as their stage started down Dalzell Canyon, but they passed through without incident. Sharp cared more for high volume and low risk. He wasn't interested in stages carrying bullion and shotgun-armed messengers.

Two and one half months later, on the night of August 30, passengers were whooping it up on the southbound stage as it dropped down toward the stage station in Coal Valley, where it would start ascending Dalzell Canyon. Above the noise, driver George Finney heard a rifle shot and a bullet whizzing overhead. He reported the incident to the station. Men sent out to investigate found tracks where a man wearing a size six boot had waited for some time for the stage to approach.

Just five days later, the southbound stage, again driven by twice-robbed Chamberlain, was stopped in Dalzell Canyon by Sharp and Dow, wearing masks. They told the passengers to sit on the ground as they rifled the express box.

"We didn't get much," Dow said. "Shall we go through the passengers?"

Three hours later, when Chamberlain met the northbound stage, he told its two Wells Fargo messengers, Mike Tovey and Tom Woodruff, about being robbed. When that stage reached the scene of the earlier robbery, Tovey found tracks going north along the stage road. His stage continued, stopping now and then for Tovey to check the tracks in the moonlight. When they reached a fork in the road, he stepped down to search the ground carefully. Then Tovey heard a voice call out, "You son of a bitch. You thought you'd sneak up on us, didn't you?"

A shot rang out and a bullet whizzed over Tovey's head to kill one of the stage's horses. "If you fellows fire, we'll kill every one of you," Sharp called out.

"Nobody is firing any guns," Tovey said. "If you want something, come on down."

Dow stepped out of the brush, and Tovey fired, killing him instantly. Sharp, still hidden, shot Tovey through the arm. Woodruff returned the fire and thought he hit his man.

Tovey bled freely, and Woodruff and a passenger helped him down the road toward a house on Desert Creek. Driver Billy Hodge got the harness off the dead horse and tied its mate to the rear of the stage. With the two messengers gone and the driver occupied, Sharp, who had not been hit after all, stepped out of the brush. He walked past his dead partner, and calmly ordered Hodge to hand over the express box. When Sharp had it, he disappeared into the darkness.

For a week, detectives, Wells Fargo messengers, and Indian trackers combed the hills. They found two men who were soon released, but no one else. Then Jim Hume, Wells Fargo's greatest detective and one of the best in the West, took over. He dug up the buried Dow. The man had small feet and he wore size six boots, but Hume did not recognize him. He said he found no papers, only a black, glazed oilcloth mask with places cut out for nose, eyes, and mouth.

On Saturday, September 11, just one week after Dow was killed, Hume and two San Francisco detectives went to a boarding house in San Francisco and asked the proprietor to show them to the room of her tenant who had small, dainty feet. They found stolen articles and evidence that the room was rented by Frank Dow, who used several aliases. They kept the room under surveillance, hoping the other robber would appear. At eleven o'clock that very night, Milton Sharp walked in. The detectives found two guns on him, one that had been stolen from a Wells Fargo express box. He also had $2,500 in gold coin in a money belt, certificates of deposit, and 150 shares of mining stock. He said the gun had been given to him by Dow, and he denied any involvement in stage robberies.

Sharp was returned to Aurora to stand trial. Although Hume thought the evidence was solid, Wells Fargo took no chances. They hired famed lawyer Pat Reddy to assist the prosecution. The trial started Thursday, October 28. The case went to the jury the next day. They found Sharp guilty on Saturday. Sentencing was set for November 10 to allow time for a second trial of assault to commit murder for the shooting of messenger Mike Tovey. Sharp returned to jail.

He didn't stay long. Thoroughly depressed about hooking up with a partner who was so naive that he stepped out in the open on the assurance that he wouldn't be shot, Sharp pondered his future. He expected a heavy sentence from the conviction he already had, and he still faced another trial. What could he do with his hands and feet shackled and a heavy ball chained to the foot shackles? He borrowed a penknife from the jailer and began carving toys for the jailer's children. Then he started digging into the 3-inch brick wall of his cell. On November 2—the very day the *Bodie Daily Free Press* mentioned that "the heavy sentence that probably awaits him has given him such a fit of blues that even the jailer scarcely knows him"—his cell was found empty. He had dug a hole through the brick wall and escaped.

All Aurora felt shock. Not because Sharp had dug through the wall; other inmates had done that. But Milton Sharp, with a fifteen-pound ball chained to his shackled ankles, had escaped on the national Election Day when thousands of people came to the courthouse to vote. How Sharp escaped through those crowds is still a mystery.

Sharp had a half-hour head start by the time the jailer learned he was missing. It took another hour to organize a posse. Sharp hobbled to the southeast over Middle Hill, toward Adobe Meadows. He stopped at Five Mile Springs, about 5 miles from Aurora. There, he pounded on his leg irons with rocks gripped in his handcuffed hands until the rivets fell out. Freed from the leg shackles, he kept moving south and east, and on Sunday, five days after his escape, he reached Candelaria, a mining town 45 miles from Aurora.

Sharp couldn't travel in a straight line because the country swarmed with men seeking the large award offered for his capture. The November nights were cold, and Sharp had nothing to eat for the five days. He could have broken into miner's cabins for food, but burglary was beneath his dignity. He continued working his way south and east.

When he reached Candelaria, Sharp stumbled to the rear of McKisseck's Saloon. He looked up at the dim light shining from the window of Dobe Willoughby's faro bank in the saloon's back room. Willoughby had been in the Aurora jail for a short time while Sharp was there, and Sharp considered him a friend. Cold to the bones from five days of exposure and weakened from the exertion of pounding off the ball and shackle and surviving five days with no food and little sleep, he huddled in the darkness. What chance did he have? He had always fought fairly. He had never shot a Wells Fargo man until that day he shot at the man who had gunned his partner down in treachery. Throughout the five days, he had been constantly surrounded by armed men, combing the hills in their search. Would he ever see his family again? These questions filled what was left of his numbed mind. Finally, he reached down, clawed a few pebbles from the frozen ground, and, using his last strength, tossed them at the window.

Tossing pebbles at a window was recognized in the West as a signal of desperation. Someone outside needed help from a friend. One of the faro players said, "Maybe that's Sharp needing help."

Men from five counties had joined the search. The state's leading newspaper had its editor there. Wells Fargo had offered a big reward. The sheriff, the governor, and the county commissioners offered additional rewards. The fifteen-pound ball and shackle had been found, and the area swarmed with searching men, but Dobe Willoughby kept on dealing faro.

Deputy Sheriff Alex McLean heard about the pebble signal, and he said it was probably Sharp. But he made no move to go out in the darkness and face the lone fugitive. Other men mocked McLean's lack of courage, but they showed no desire, themselves, to go out in the dark and see who threw the pebbles.

Finally, a miner entered another saloon and said there was a man outside who said he wanted to talk to an officer. Word got to McLean, and he mustered up enough courage to meet the mysterious visitor. Approaching with his drawn pistol, he first asked if Sharp was armed. Sharp had no weapon.

Sharp still wore the handcuffs. After McLean adjusted them to stop the hurting, Sharp asked for something to eat. McLean took him to Billy Coalter's chop-stand, where he devoured a huge meal. Then, McLean took his prisoner to the Wells Fargo office for safe keeping until he could make arrangements to return him to Aurora. There, Drury Wells, editor of the *Territorial Enterprise*, interviewed him.

Sharp told Wells that he would never have surrendered without a fight if he'd only had a gun. He said he had worn the shackle for three days. All that time, he was surrounded by armed men hunting for him.

"It seemed to me," he said, "that I could not get out of their sight. The shackle hurt my ankle and made me very lame. I am not well acquainted in this part of the country. I don't know exactly where I went in my travels. I had to change my course every few miles to avoid the men who were tracking me. I concluded to come here and try to find a friend that I thought would help me. But I didn't find him, and I didn't like to ask for him."

Wells thought Sharp a "mild-mannered, pleasant-spoken fellow, but with a flash now and then beneath the surface which showed him alert and keen as a steel trap." He was not inclined to be communicative at first. When Wells asked how he got the shackle off his leg, he only said, "Well, I got it off, and I was glad of it."

Sharp went back to Aurora to be locked securely in an iron cell. Three days later, the judge sentenced him to twenty years in the state prison. The other indictments were dismissed. Jim Hume and the two Wells Fargo messengers, Mike Tovey and Tom Woodruff, delivered Sharp to the Nevada State Prison in Carson. (Three years later Jim Hume would capture Black Bart, an even more famous stage robber.) When their stage arrived, other passengers described Sharp as "a perfect gentleman in manners and conversation."

Sharp was not a good prisoner for his first year in prison. In May 1881, he had a ball and chain applied for making tools in an attempt to escape. In August he went to the dungeon for stealing a file and concealing it on his person. On November 24, six months after the ball and chain were applied, the ball was removed. One month later, on Christmas Eve, the chain was removed.

Then, Sharp behaved himself. In 1887, after seven years in prison, his request for pardon was denied. A year later, it was denied again. Sharp had become a trusty, with special privileges. He felt he had no hope for release, so he abused his privileges and escaped in August 1889.

We don't know what he did for the next four years, but on October 3, 1893, Sharp drove into a livery stable in Red Bluff, California, with a farmer for whom he worked. He came face to face with a former convict he had known in prison. They both recognized each other. Neither spoke, and Sharp did not think it necessary to ask the other man to not betray him. A few minutes later, while trying on a new pair of boots, Sharp looked up to see the sheriff. He had again been deceived, this time by a man he thought a friend.

Back in prison, Sharp wrote a long and detailed letter to Wells Fargo's Jim Hume. He listed names and addresses of those for whom he had worked during his four years of liberty. Hume interviewed those persons and decided that Sharp had made every effort to rehabilitate himself. Apparently, he had avoided contact with all his old associates, for the prison had received a note from a former friend that Sharp had drowned in a California flood.

Hume wrote to Nevada authorities, reporting his findings, and urging that Sharp's next application for pardon be granted. Sharp filed a new petition in May 1894, and Governor Roswell Colcord pardoned him the following July.

We don't know where Milton Sharp went or what he did, but apparently he resumed his good habits and continued to shun his one bad one—stage robbery. Betrayed by two men, one of them a friend, he was finally rescued by his old nemesis, Wells Fargo's greatest detective.

Ben Kuhl

A Nevada Tragedy

Besides providing the West's first train robbery, Nevada gave us the West's last holdup of a horse-drawn stage. And the resulting murder trial became a United States landmark in the development of admissible criminal evidence.

Jarbidge hardly seemed part of Nevada. The stage road came southwest from Rogerson, Idaho, through increasingly rough country, crossing the state line 8 miles north of town. Snowdrifts up to 30 feet deep made Jarbidge the most isolated mining camp in Nevada. Jarbidge's name came from an Indian word for Devil. Yet it had become the state's leading producer of gold in the years leading up to the First World War.

The December 5, 1916, evening stage from Rogerson, due in Jarbidge between 5:00 and 6:30, was late to no one's surprise. Snow had been falling heavily since midafternoon, and with the plunging temperature, the freezing wind, and the precarious descent into the narrow Jarbidge River canyon, no one expected driver Fred Searcey to be on time. But at 9 P.M., Postmaster Scott Fleming, anxious about his mail, started asking questions. He learned from Rose Dexter, who lived at the north end of town a half mile from the post office, that she had heard a loud crack, "like a high powered gun" at about 6:30 that evening. Shortly after, the stage passed with two men sitting on the seat. One of the men seemed slumped over, and the other had his overcoat collar turned up around his ears. Knowing Searcey well, Rose hollered, "Halloo," but did not get an answer. The stage disappeared in the darkness, and she thought no more about it.

"I thought it might be someone shooting a mad coyote," Rose said about the noise she had heard.

Ben Kuhl
Nevada Historical Society, Reno

A hastily summoned search party, carrying kerosene lanterns, found the stage in a dense willow thicket, its horses tied to a tree. The stage was just 200 yards off the road and a quarter mile from the business part of the town. Fred Searcey lay dead on the seat, a bullet wound behind his left ear and a gaping exit wound in his mouth and right cheek. Frozen blood had caked on the seat and floor, and the horses shivered from the cold. The second-class mail sack had been ripped open and its contents strewn about. The first-class sack, in which cash was sometimes sent, was missing. The storm raged too much to continue the search, but guards were posted on all trails to make sure no one left, and the citizens waited until daylight.

The next morning, fairly certain that the killer was still among the 1,500 residents of the town, Constable I. C. Hill and Justice of the Peace J.A. Yewell organized a new search party. It included J.B. McCormick, an experienced hunter. McCormick saw dog tracks near the stage and examined them carefully. He blew out the new snow and got a good print in the old snow underneath.

"I believe these tracks were made by one of them old tramp dogs that don't really belong to nobody," he said. "Let's keep our eyes open and see what we can see. Maybe the dog will come back."

"Well, he's a big one," another said. "Could be that big yeller one that hangs around that rounder name of Ben Kuhl."

"That one on a peace bond for jumping a claim?" someone asked.

"Yep. He's a tough one, I hear."

"They say he's served time in California," another said.

"Hell, he's also done state prison time in Oregon."

Sure enough, at about ten o'clock, one of the camp's dogs came by as though following a trail. McCormick and the others watched and followed as the dog went directly to a place in the brush, about 20 feet off the trail, where the fresh-fallen snow still covered the missing first-class mail sack. They dug it up. By then, they knew that it had contained $2,800 in cash being mailed to the Success Bar and Cafe to cash checks.

The cash was gone, but a bloody palm print had been left behind on a torn letter.

"Anybody recognize the dog?" someone asked.

"Seen him around with that Kuhl."

"Let's tell the sheriff."

The search party also found where the killer had waited for the stage, evidently jumping on it as it went past. Footprints and the dog tracks led through the trees and across a bridge. There they found a blood-soaked overcoat, a sack of coins, another sack of registered mail, and a shirt and bandana weighted down with stones in the stream. The shirt resembled those usually worn by Kuhl, and it had the letter "K" marked with ink, immediately below the collar. It appeared to have been washed to get rid of blood.

When Justice of the Peace Yewell confronted Kuhl with the overcoat, Kuhl said, "I never owned an overcoat in my life. I wear a mackinaw." But the coat belonged to a friend of his and would have been available for him to wear. In fact some citizens said they had seen Kuhl wearing it.

Kuhl was not popular. He had been a cook at the OK Mine for about a month, but was fired when he tried to jump another man's claim. Now, he did odd jobs in the camp while waiting for his trespassing trial. He lived in a floored tent with some other drifters. Already known as a troublemaker for the claim-jumping incident, he had previously served a year in the Oregon State Prison for animal larceny and four months in the Yuba County, California, jail for petty theft.

"I hear he needed money," someone said.

"Yeah, to hire a lawyer and to pay a fine for the claim jumping if he gets off that easy."

"He's got more to worry about now."

A search of the tent Kuhl shared with Ed Beck and Billy McGraw produced a .44 caliber revolver, the hammer resting on the one spent cartridge. The gun, found under Kuhl's bed, belonged to Beck, who said he had loaned it to McGraw. The night of the killing, Beck had asked

McGraw for the gun, saying Kuhl wanted it for hunting. McGraw delivered the gun to Beck. Kuhl and Beck were seen in the Success Bar and Cafe at about eight o'clock, shortly before Searcey's body was found. They had bought a round of drinks and seemed to be drawing attention to their presence in the bar and to the time.

It took two days for Elko County Sheriff Joe Harris and District Attorney Edward P. Carville to come from the county seat. They had to ride trains east to Ogden, Utah, north to Pocatello, Idaho, and west to Twin Falls, where they changed to the stage. A few men provided Kuhl with an alibi, but he, Beck, and McGraw were arrested and charged with murder.

Kuhl, a 5-foot, 11-inch, slender man with light blue eyes was thirty-three. A native of Indiana, he had a wife and an infant son in Salt Lake City, and had been in Jarbidge about four months.

Beck, also thirty-three, was a native of Finland and had been in town only a week. Although he had been in the United States for fifteen years, he could barely speak English. He was a heavy drinker.

The trial was originally set for April 16, 1917. But Jarbidge continued to suffer through one of the worst winters in its history. On April 3, Carville and Harris again made the long trip to collect evidence and check on witnesses. They returned to Elko and asked the court to postpone the trial to September. Edwin E. Caine had been appointed by the court to defend Kuhl. Judge Erroll Taber agreed that the defendants could be tried separately, and he set Kuhl's trial for September 18, with Beck's to follow. He asked the press to not report Kuhl's trial as it might prejudice the jurors selected for Beck's case.

District Attorney Carville prosecuted the cases. C.H. Stone, supervisor of the Federal Bureau of Investigation in Bakersfield, California, was the most important of his forty-six witnesses. Stone, a fingerprint expert, identified the palm print found on the envelope as that of Kuhl. Many people testified that they had seen Kuhl wearing the overcoat that had been found near the river.

The jury found Kuhl guilty on October 7, 1917, after eighteen days of trial and two hours of deliberations.

Beck's trial began on October 8. He testified in his own defense. He said that Kuhl had told him that he and Searcey had arranged a frame-up in which it would appear that Kuhl was holding up the stage. He needed a gun to carry out his part. Kuhl and Searcey were to divide the proceeds of the false holdup between them. Beck said that he got the gun from McGraw and gave it to Kuhl. After the crime Kuhl had told Beck that Searcey would not go through with the deal and he, Kuhl, had "bumped him off." Kuhl also told Beck that he had taken about $2,000 and would split it with Beck if Beck kept quiet about what Kuhl had told him.

McGraw also testified in Beck's trial that he gave the gun to Beck on his original understanding that Beck and Kuhl wanted the revolver to go deer hunting. Later he learned about the simulated holdup.

Beck was also found guilty. McGraw's trial was scheduled to be the last. After he testified against Kuhl and Beck, his charges were dropped.

Beck was sentenced to life imprisonment; Kuhl, to death. The convicted man had a right to choose between hanging and shooting, and Kuhl chose to be shot. The court set his execution date for January 18, 1918. That date was changed from time to time as Kuhl appealed his conviction.

The Nevada Supreme Court decided Kuhl's appeal on September 5, 1918. Kuhl's lawyer pointed out that no court in any English-speaking country of the world had ever allowed palm prints into evidence. The court affirmed the conviction, and the new execution date was December 20, 1918.

One week before the execution date, Kuhl persuaded the State Board of Pardons to look into his claim that he had acted in self-defense. He told the board that the robbery was a frame-up between him and Searcey. He said that some time before the crime, he had told Searcey that he needed money to develop some mining claims. Searcey then told him that he had previously arranged a false holdup in Idaho and had gotten away with it. They agreed to wait until money was being sent to a Jarbidge bar to cash checks and then work the false holdup. They agreed that Searcey would delay the arrival of the stage to give Kuhl enough time to stash the plunder and get to the post office before the stage arrived, so he would have an alibi.

Kuhl said they rehearsed the holdup once at the selected point, about a mile and one half from Jarbidge. On the night of the crime, he met the stage at the agreed point. He and Searcey sat on the box and discussed the "job" as they moved toward the town.

Kuhl said that Searcey told him that a sack in the stage boot held $300 and there was $2,800 in greenbacks in the first-class mail sack. Searcey was willing to give up the $300, but he refused to cut the mail sack open and give up the greenbacks.

An argument followed, and Kuhl claimed that Searcey went for his gun. Believing that he had been double-crossed and that his own life was in danger, Kuhl then shot Searcey, grabbing his body to keep it from falling off the stage. That, he claimed, is how his clothing became bloody.

Kuhl held Searcey's body up as the stage passed Mrs. Dexter's house, where she called out to them. After he tied the horses in the willow thicket, Kuhl took the first-class mail sack into the brush, where he removed the $2,800. Then he washed up, made his way back to his tent, and joined the search party looking for the missing stage. In fact he helped take Searcey down from the box and was not sure until then that he had actually killed the man.

On December 13, by a vote of three to two, the board of pardons commuted Kuhl's sentence from execution to life imprisonment. The acting governor, the attorney general, and Chief Justice Patrick McCarran of the state supreme court voted to commute. The two associate justices of the supreme court opposed.

The Reno *Gazette*, claiming "inside facts," said the first vote was to not commute, the chief justice siding with his two associates. Then he changed his mind. The Reno *Gazette* also claimed that the evidence produced at the trial supported Kuhl's story before the board of pardons.

Beck was paroled in 1923, after serving six years of his life sentence.

Kuhl came up regularly for parole during the 1920s and 1930s, and was regularly turned down. For twelve years, he was in charge of the prison bake shop, during which time he took a master baker's course by mail from the Chicago School of Technology. He also studied music and directed the prison orchestra for three years.

In an April 21, 1936, letter to the governor, Kuhl's expression is an impressive witness of the change in his life since he had so brutally murdered Fred Searcey almost twenty years before. He wrote:

> "For the last eight years my duties have been with the prison library. Our present collection of literature comprises some of the most cherished gems of ancient lore. I worked unceasingly for years before my labors were rewarded. Now we have a total of five thousand volumes, obtained through popular subscription from the many good people of our state, and we are indeed proud and sincerely grateful to every one who has contributed to this most worthy cause.
>
> "Our greatest achievement has been the inauguration of our Prison School, and we trust that this program may be adequately supported by our Legislature and made a permanent policy of the institution."

Over seventy citizens of the Carson City area signed a petition at this time, asking that Kuhl be granted parole. Wardens and other prison officials added their letters in support of Kuhl's petitions. [One such warden, Carl Hocker, was later captain of the security staff at San Quentin and a friend of this writer when, as a deputy district attorney for Marin County, California, he prosecuted cases arising in that prison.] No one ever mentioned any behavioral problems. But Kuhl's prison folder contained a letter from prosecutor Carville, by then a district judge, reminding the parole board that he considered the original death sentence completely appropriate. He thought the reduction to a life sentence was all the mercy the state owed Ben Kuhl.

Kuhl's prison folder contained many letters from his wife and his mother. His mother had married again and lived in Kalamazoo, Michigan. His father lived in Walla Walla, Washington. Kuhl's wife Minnie, short for Minnier, divorced him after his conviction, but her second marriage must have ended because she resumed using the Kuhl name in her letters. On November 3, 1927, she wrote the governor, enclosing a letter she had recently received from Kuhl.

This letter, dated October 8, 1927, started this way: "My darling Minnie: At last your long wanted letter reached me. My goodness, Pet, I just knew something was terribly wrong. You poor, dear kid, I really am sorry for you. Yes, sweetheart it seems as though all our sorrows come at once. But try to be cheerful; there will be better times surely some day. I think you have done so wonderful all these years. God bless you; I am proud of you. And my little man was sick, too. My that is tough. But glad to know he is better."

Minnie ended her letter to the governor: "It is not my idea to make an extended plea for mercy, but I do so hope you may feel that justice has been served and that more good will come to three of us from his liberation than from his continued confinement."

Mrs. Kuhl also included a letter from her son to the governor. These remarks suggest that most of the letter was written by Minnie and copied by the boy:

"I have always loved my Papa Ben, as I remember him. He has been in the Nevada State Prison about eleven years now, and it seems that I don't know what a father's love is since he left us so many years ago.

"I know my papa wasn't a bad man or criminal. He just got in with rough associates and they influenced him to do wrong. It seems that things have just gone entirely wrong in the last few years. My mother has just been under a very serious operation, and she is in need of someone to help her out. She is worried about the home and she thinks it is liable to be taken away from us. This winter she knows will be a very hard one for us unless Papa Ben could come home to help us, and help cheer my mother because God only knows her worries, needs, and sorrows.

"I work as much as possible in the summer and after school so I can help my mother. I am trying to get an education, trying to grasp the present opportunities but unless Papa Ben comes home I'm afraid I'll have to give up.

"I know that your decision will be for the best, because only efficient and capable men are chosen to be at the head of any state's executive department. I shall certainly appreciate your kind consideration and trouble and more power to Nevada's State executive, Governor Fred B. Balzar."

Eighteen years later, on May 7, 1945, Ben Kuhl finally got his parole. He was sixty-one, the oldest inmate in the prison and the inmate who had served the longest time. The parole certificate was signed by the attorney general, two justices of the state supreme court, and by the head of the board, Edward Carville, then the state governor. The parole contained the special condition that Kuhl leave Nevada and never return.

But Kuhl's "better times" never came. We don't know what happened. Some say Kuhl went to California where he soon died of disease. Others say he was hitchhiking toward northeastern Nevada when he was struck and killed by an unidentified hit-and-run driver. The latter story is more likely true, as he had promised the parole board that he would remarry his wife if released. She and their son still lived in Salt Lake City.

Perhaps the boy learned that Papa Ben was an unpopular claim jumper and petty thief who brutally killed an acquaintance. But perhaps he also learned that his father improved his life through self-education and community work inside a prison until free citizens and prison officials joined in his request for parole. The district attorney who'd worked to convict Kuhl in a landmark evidential case was the same man who, as governor, paroled him.

——⋗●⋖—— Bibliography ——⋗●⋖——

Sam Brown

Brown, George R., ed. *Reminiscences of Senator William M. Stewart.* New York: Neale Publishing, 1908.

Sacramento Daily Union, July 8, 10, 1861.

Virginia City Territorial Enterprise, March 3, 1860.

Van Sickle, Elona. "The Death of Sam Brown," 1932 manuscript, ND 161, Nevada Historical Society, Reno.

Van Sickle, H. "Utah Desperadoes," dictated manuscript in Bancroft Library, Berkeley, California. Filed in Nevada Historical Society papers, 1913-1914, v. 1.

Van Sickle, Henry. 1883 Manuscript, Nevada Historical Society, Reno.

Bill Mayfield

Nevada Democrat, January 2, 1862.

Sacramento *Bee*, November 26, 1861.

Sacramento *Union*, November 23, 25, 1861; March 17, 1862; June 26, 1863.

San Francisco *Chronicle*, January 24, 1892.

Virginia City Territorial Enterprise, August 10, 1861.

Langford Farner Peel

Curtis, Warren R. "The Passing of Farmer Peel" in *Pony Express Courier*, May, 1943.

Elko Daily Independent. January 10, 1877; November 6, 1897.

Gillis, William R. *Gold Rush Days with Mark Twain*. New York: Albert and Charles Boni, 1930.

Gold Hill Daily News. October 26, 28, 29, 1863.

Virginia Evening Chronicle, January 4, 1877.

John Richard "Rattlesnake Dick" Darling

Folder 0004, Box NSP 0001. Nevada State Archives.

Nevada State Journal, August 25, 1883.

Virginia City Evening Bulletin, September 14, 15, 1863.

Virginia City Territorial Enterprise, May 16, 26, 27, 30, July 1, 1866; November 15, 1872.

Bravery at Bullion Bend

Gold Hill Daily News, June 29, 30, 1864.

Sacramento Union, July 2, 7, 1864.

San Francisco Alta California, July 27, August 27, 1864.

Nevada Appeal, March 12, 1978.

John Moriarty

Gracey, Charles. "Early Days in Lincoln County," in *First Biennial Report of the Nevada Historical Society*, Carson City: State Printing Office, 1909.

Pioche Daily Record, September 22, 24, 1872; August 2, 3, 5, 1873.

Reese River Revielle, August 4, 1873.

Virginia City Territorial Enterprise, November 15, 1868.

Train of Destiny

Elko Chronicle, November 10, 13, 1870.

Gold Hill Daily News, November 5, 7, 8, 10, 11, 12, 14, 1870.

Folders 0073, 0083. Box NSP 0001. Nevada State Library and Archives.

Andrew Jackson "Big Jack" Davis

Eureka Daily Sentinel, September 5, 6, 7, 9, 1877.

Virginia City Territorial Enterprise, November 1, 1866; December 16, 1870; September 5, 9, 1877.

Prison Riot

Folders 0020, 0034, 0078, Box NSP 0001. Nevada State Library and Archives.

Virginia City Territorial Enterprise, September 19, 21, 22, 28, 29; October 19, 31, 1871.

Nicanor Rodrigues

Block, Eugene B. *Great Stagecoach Robbers of the West.* Garden City: Doubleday & Co., 1962.

Drury, Wells. *An Editor on the Comstock Lode.* Palo Alto: Pacific Books, 1936.

Sacramento Daily Union, April 24, 1856.

Milton Sharp

Dillon, Richard. *Wells Fargo Detective, A Biography of James B. Hume.* Reno: University of Nevada Press, 1986.

Drury, Wells. *An Editor on the Comstock Lode.* Palo Alto: Pacific Books, 1936.

Reno Evening Gazette, September 6, 1880.

Virginia Chronicle, September 11, 1880.

Weekly Nevada State Journal, September 11, 18, 1880.

Ben Kuhl

Carson City News, December 14, 1918.

Elko Daily Free Press, December 6, 1916.

Elko Daily Independent, December 12, 13, 1916.

Nevada State Journal, May 9, 1945.

Nevada State Prison inmate case file 2018, Ben Kuhl. Nevada State Library and Archives.

Reno Evening Gazette, December 10, 1918.

Virginia City Chronicle, December 11, 1918.

About the Author

Charles L. "Chuck" Convis grew up on a North Dakota farm. He left home at sixteen to work on steam railroads in Wyoming and Utah, graduating from high school in Cheyenne. After a season on a halibut boat in the Gulf of Alaska, he joined the Marines at seventeen, fighting at Iwo Jima. He has two engineering degrees from the University of Texas. After working as a land surveyor for a Texas oil company, he entered Harvard Law School, where he received the Wall Street Journal Student Achievement Award and graduated in 1956.

His thirty-nine-year career in law included foreign oil exploration, teaching law in Texas and Pennsylvania, and serving in two California district attorney offices. During his last assignment he specialized in prosecuting murder cases. He also has a Ph. D. in psychology and has published in law and psychology.

Chuck is the biographer of Myles Keogh of Indian Wars fame (*The Honor of Arms*, Westernlore Press, Tucson, 1990) and has published in a variety of western journals and magazines. His work has been reprinted in *Voices in Fiction and Nonfiction*. He also writes and self-publishes a series of true, short sketches about the Old West, which now numbers thirty-two titles (Pioneer Press, Carson City).

Chuck and Mary Anne, his wife of fifty-seven years, retired to Carson City eleven years ago. They have five children and fifteen grandchildren, ranging in age from a few months to sixteen. He enjoys bridge, Elderhostel travel abroad, skiing, writing, and visiting grandchildren.

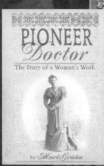